Alessandro Stradella

Esule dalle sfere

Early Musical Masterworks—Critical Editions and Commentaries

GENERAL EDITORS
Howard E. Smither
Vincent Duckles
Charles Hamm

Orazio Vecchi's "L'Amfiparnaso,"
edited by Cecil Adkins

Josquin des Prez's "Missa Pange lingua,"
edited by Thomas Warburton

Marc-Antoine Charpentier's "Pestis Mediolanensis,"
edited by H. Wiley Hitchcock

Michel-Richard Delalande's "De profundis,"
edited by James R. Anthony

Giovanni Battista Sammartini's "Sonate a tre stromenti,"
edited by Bathia Churgin

Alessandro Stradella's "Esule dalle sfere,"
edited by Eleanor F. McCrickard

Alessandro Stradella

Esule dalle sfere

A Cantata for the Souls of Purgatory

An Edition with Commentary
by Eleanor F. McCrickard

Italian Text Transcribed and Translated
by Aldo Scaglione

The University of North Carolina Press · Chapel Hill

Cut on cover and title page:
First page of Angelo's aria "Sù, sù, spariscano"
(Turin, Biblioteca Nazionale Universitaria,
Giordano 12, fol. 122v). Grateful acknowledgment is
made to the Biblioteca Nazionale Universitaria for
permission to reproduce this manuscript page and to
Dott.ssa Piera Bouvet for assistance in obtaining a
photograph of it.

Music autography by Helen Jenner

© 1983 The University of North Carolina Press

All rights reserved

Manufactured in the United States of America

Library of Congress Cataloging in Publication Data

Stradella, Alessandro, 1644–1682.
Esule dalle sfere.

(Early musical masterworks)
For solo voices (SB), chorus (SATB), 2 violins,
and continuo.
Libretto attributed to Pompeo Figari.
Edited from mss. in the Biblioteca Nazionale
Universitaria, Turin (Giordano 12) and the Biblioteca
Estense, Modena (Mus. F. 1148).
Blank staff for realization of figured bass.
Libretto with English translation: p.
Bibliography: p.
Includes index.
1. Cantatas, Sacred—Scores. I. McCrickard,
Eleanor F. II. Scaglione, Aldo D. III. Figari,
Pompeo, fl. 1690. IV. Series. V. Title.
M2020.S87E8 1983   82-17544
ISBN 0-8078-1536-5

To Don

Contents

Acknowledgments	ix
Abbreviations	xi
Alessandro Stradella and His Cantatas	3
Pompeo Figari and His Poems	6
The Work in Historical Context: Cantata and Oratorio	9
Structure and Style	16
Recitatives	16
Arias	17
Choruses	18
Instrumental Sections	18
The Performance of *Esule dalle sfere*	20
Selection of Instruments	20
Realization of the Continuo	22
Selection of Voices	26
Vocal and Instrumental Ornamentation	26
Tempo, Dynamics, and Articulation	28
The Present Edition	29
Sources	29
Editorial Procedures	30
Textual Comments and Variants	31
Text of *Esule dalle sfere*	33
Score of *Esule dalle sfere*	39
Bibliography	139
Index	143

Acknowledgments

I wish to thank numerous individuals and groups whose generous help has contributed to the completion of this edition: Dott.ssa Piera Bouvet of the Biblioteca Nazionale Universitaria in Turin and Dott.ssa Silvana Verdini of the Biblioteca Estense in Modena, who made the sources available; Early Musical Masterworks Series editors at the University of North Carolina at Chapel Hill, Professor Emeritus William S. Newman, who was particularly encouraging in early stages, and Professor Howard E. Smither, who offered invaluable comments throughout the project; Professor Aldo Scaglione of the University of North Carolina at Chapel Hill, who provided the expertise necessary to solve many problems in the transcription and translation of the text; and the Research Council at the University of North Carolina at Greensboro, which provided generous financial support.

I am also particularly grateful to my colleague, Professor Richard Cox, for directing the Chamber Singers in the first performance of *Esule dalle sfere* in its entirety. A successful earlier performance of the three soprano arias by Florence Peacock, Joyce Peck, and I Musici di Cappella della Collina under the direction of Mary Frances Boyce in Chapel Hill encouraged me to pursue further an edition of the work.

Many others contributed in a number of ways: my colleagues—Professors Carol Marsh, Aubrey Garlington, Eddie Bass, Phyllis Tektonidis, Nancy Fogarty, and Margo Bender—and student assistants—Gil Fray, Mark Neville, Hannah Raymer, and Edward Stanley. Finally, I am grateful to my mother, Professor Elizabeth T. Fowler of Maryville College, who provided needed advice at many stages, and to my husband, Professor Donald L. McCrickard, without whose helpful criticism, understanding, and support the edition would not have been possible.

Eleanor F. McCrickard
Greensboro, North Carolina
November 1982

Abbreviations

GB/Lbm	Great Britain/London, British Museum	I/Rli	Italy/Rome, Biblioteca dell'Accademia Nazionale dei Lincei e Corsiniana
GB/Cfm	Great Britain/Cambridge, Fitzwilliam Museum	I/Tn	Italy/Turin, Biblioteca Nazionale Universitaria
I/Bc	Italy/Bologna, Civico Museo Bibliografico Musicale	I/Vnm	Italy/Venice, Biblioteca Nazionale Marciana
I/MOe	Italy/Modena, Biblioteca Estense		
I/Nc	Italy/Naples, Biblioteca del Conservatorio		

Alessandro Stradella

Esule dalle sfere

Alessandro Stradella and His Cantatas

Alessandro Stradella's life is difficult to reconstruct because relatively few facts are known. In the past, certain aspects of his life have stimulated the imaginations of writers of dramas, poems, operas, novels, and songs.[1] However, fantasy and fact were so entwined, especially during the nineteenth century, that it became difficult to distinguish between the two. Recent attempts to provide accurate accounts of the composer's life have led to certain definite conclusions, although many gaps in his biography still exist.[2]

Stradella, once thought to be a Roman, was born in Nepi, near Viterbo, in the year 1639.[3] His ancestors were prosperous, well-educated Tuscans—doctors, lawyers, and clergy. Stradella remained in Nepi for several years but at some point went to Bologna for a period of time and possibly later to Florence. Stradella's teachers are not known. However, the Bologna area was rich with music activity in the decades of the fifties and sixties. Stradella was there part of this time, and he undoubtedly knew the work of Maurizio Cazzati (ca. 1620–77), maestro di cappella of the famous San Petronio church. Some eighty years after Stradella's death, Francesco Maria Veracini (1690–1768) notes that Stradella was a student of Ercole Bernabei (1620–87),[4] a Roman master of the *stile antico* and maestro di cappella at San Marcello.

Recent investigations indicate the first documented evidence of Stradella in Rome is his now lost Latin oratorio composed in 1667 for the Arciconfraternità del Santissimo Crocifisso at San Marcello.[5] Between 1667 and 1676, Stradella was clearly in Rome, where he enjoyed the patronage of some of the most famous personages in Rome, including Queen Christina of Sweden (who resided there and was an important patron of music) and the Colonna family. Numerous well-documented works come from the Roman period, including music for the Teatro Tordinona[6] and the oratorio *San Giovanni Battista*, which was included in a series of oratorios at San Giovanni dei Fiorentini during Holy Year 1675.[7]

Stradella left Rome permanently in 1677 for several reasons. He was forced out of work at the theater because Innocent XI suppressed theatrical activity shortly after he ascended to the papacy in the fall of 1676, thus sending many who depended on the theater out of town. Furthermore, Stradella was involved in a scandal that incited the ire of Cardinal Alderan Cibo.[8]

Subsequently, Stradella's professional career and his escapades with women became inextricable. He went from Rome to Venice, where he stayed only a short time but long enough to persuade a lady student of his to accompany him to Turin. The first attempt on his life was made on 10 October 1677 by representatives of an offended Venetian gentleman associated with Stradella's lady friend. As a result,

---

1. For an extensive list, see Jander, "Works of Stradella Related to the Cantata and the Opera," pp. 3–4.
2. Results of the recent archival discoveries will appear in *Atti del convegno internazionale Alessandro Stradella: Siena 1982*, a volume of *Chigiana* currently in press, and will include the following pertinent articles: Patrizia Radicchi, "La famiglia Stradella e i suoi rapporti con la Toscana"; Lorenzo Bianconi, "Committenza pubblica e committanza privata: Alessandro Stradella da Roma a Genova"; Mercedes Viale Ferrero, "Alessandro Stradella a Torino"; and Eleanora Simi Bonini, "Stradella negli archivi romani." For recent discoveries, also see two articles by Carolyn Gianturco, "La famiglia Stradella: nouvi documenti biografici," forthcoming in *Nuova rivista musicale italiana*, and a brief biographical sketch, "Stradella: True Biography." All information concerning recent research will be discussed by Gianturco in a study of Stradella for Oxford University Press. See also older studies by Owen Jander, "Stradella," in *MGG*, 12: cols. 1418–22; and Gianturco, "Stradella," in the *New Grove*, 18:188–93.
3. The recent archival discoveries have negated much of Giazotto's *Vita*, which places Stradella in Rome for a large portion of his life. Since church records for Nepi were burned by French troops in 1798, the new birth date has been deduced by Gianturco from other notary records in Nepi and Viterbo.

4. Gianturco, "Stradella: True Biography," p. 757.
5. Veracini, "Il trionfo della pratica musicali," p. 377.
6. Cametti, *Il teatro di Tordinona*, 2:323, 327, 330, 334, 335.
7. Casimiri, "Oratorii," p. 160.
8. Pitoni, "Stradella," pp. 699–700; and Bianconi, "Committenza pubblica e committanza privata."

Stradella had to leave Turin quickly for Genoa, where he had the patronage, at least part of the time, of Anton Brignole-Sale, one of its leading citizens. Several of Stradella's most important works were written at this time, including *Il barcheggio*,[9] which he composed for the wedding of his patron's daughter. Once again, however, Stradella became involved with a young lady, this one from the powerful Lomellini family of Genoa. Her brothers came to the defense of her honor and had Stradella murdered in the Piazza Bianchi in Genoa on 25 February 1682. Thus the music world lost an excellent composer in his forty-third year. Stradella was a talented singer, violinist, and keyboard player, but his fame rests on his work as a composer. He was most prolific in the medium of the cantata.

Stradella wrote some 350 works, primarily secular vocal compositions, according to Owen Jander's monumental catalogue of Stradella's works and a more detailed index of the cantatas.[10] His works were widely disseminated throughout Europe, as is attested by the presence of manuscript copies in libraries not only in Italy (Modena, Turin, Bologna, Venice, Florence, Naples, Genoa, Rome), but also in Great Britain, France, Germany, Belgium, Austria, Denmark, Portugal, and even the United States.

Excluding cantatas, Stradella's extant works include 6 operas, 6 oratorios, 32 canzonettas, 22 madrigals, 9 serenatas, 11 prologues, 9 intermezzi, 5 miscellaneous semidramatic works, 7 substitute arias, 20 motets, and 27 instrumental works.[11]

Of the 400 cantatas attributed to Stradella, only 195 are authentic.[12] That Stradella actually wrote approximately half of these works is understandable in view of the practice of the day—since his name was prestigious, lesser composers often attached his name to their works. Of Stradella's 195 cantatas, 151, the vast majority, are for solo voice; 29 are duets; and 15 are trios.[13] *Esule dalle sfere* is classed as a duet in Jander's index of the cantatas even though in addition to the two solo voices there is also a chorus, two voices of which act in a solo capacity.

Stradella prefers the soprano voice for his solo cantatas.[14] The use of a chorus in a cantata is unusual; in fact, Jander's index lists only one, *Esule dalle sfere*. The other cantata with a chorus is the six-voice *Ah! troppo è ver*. Most cantatas, especially the solo works, are accompanied by the continuo only. Of the sixteen cantatas accompanied by more instruments, twelve employ two violins and continuo. Unusual scorings include four strings for one solo work and a duet; a violoncello (or bass viola da gamba) virtuoso part for another solo work; and one concerto grosso plus two concertino parts (situated on three wagons!) for one of the trios, also referred to as a serenata.[15]

The overwhelming majority of Stradella's cantatas are secular. Only six sacred cantatas are listed in Jander's *Catalogue*, but one of these, *Pugna certamen*, has a Latin text and does not fit into the definition of a cantata, as will be seen in a later chapter. Three of the five remaining works are larger works involving two to six voices. All are accompanied by at least two

---

9. See Bernstein, "Stradella's Serenata *Il barcheggio*"; and Gianturco, "Music for a Genoese Wedding of 1681," forthcoming in *Music and Letters*.

10. The present résumé is based on two catalogs compiled by Jander, *A Catalogue of Manuscripts of Compositions by Stradella* and a cantata index, *Alessandro Stradella*, fasc. 4 in the Wellesley Edition Cantata Index Series (WECIS). See also Gianturco's list of works in "Stradella," *New Grove*, 18:191–93.

11. Included is an additional work for keyboard not listed in the Jander *Catalogue*. See McCrickard, *Alessandro Stradella*, app. 1.

12. Because of the illusiveness of the term *cantata*, Jander had to establish criteria for the inclusion of works in WECIS. He first divided the cantatas into two groups: works clearly authentic according to source reliability and stylistic evidence and works about which there are questions of authenticity. Then he classified the works according to the number of voices: one, two, or three. Jander included in WECIS madrigals for one to three voices that were in the older *Catalogue of Manuscripts* under "madrigals." Since Gianturco's list of the cantatas in the *New Grove* includes works of more than three voices, the rest of the madrigals from the *Catalogue* are included as well as some serenatas.

13. Because it is for six voices, *Ah! troppo è ver* is not included in WECIS even though it is labeled *cantata* in the two sources. Gianturco does include the work in the *New Grove*.

14. In fact, he uses a soprano clef for 131 of the 151 solo works. Of the remaining works, 9 have alto clef, 9 bass, 1 mezzo-soprano, and 1 tenor. From source to source the clef is occasionally different, thus indicating a different voice for that particular source. In the 29 works for two voices, most are scored for soprano (or mezzo-soprano) / bass (or baritone)—16 in number, including *Esule dalle sfere*. Other combinations include 8 for soprano / soprano (1 of these possibly for soprano / tenor), 3 for soprano / alto, and 1 each for tenor / bass and mezzo-soprano / tenor. A variety of different vocal scorings is used for the 15 three-voice works. Of the 15, 8 employ soprano / soprano / bass; 4, soprano / alto / bass (1 of these possibly for soprano / alto / tenor); and 1 each, alto / tenor / bass, soprano / tenor / bass, and soprano / soprano / soprano. See Chaikin, "Solo Soprano Cantatas."

15. This serenata, *Qual prodigio è ch'io miro*, was borrowed by Handel for his *Israel in Egypt*.

violins and continuo, and one involves concerto grosso instrumentation.[16] The two cantatas with a four-part chorus are both sacred works.

> 16. In addition to *Esule dalle sfere*, other sacred cantatas listed in the *Catalogue* are *Da cuspide ferrate*, for contralto; *Crudo mar di fiamme orribili*, for bass; *Si apra al riso ogni labbro*, for soprano, contralto, and bass; *Ah! troppo è ver*, for three sopranos, contralto, tenor, and bass; and *Pugna certamen, militia est vita* (designated *dialogo*), for soprano, alto, tenor, and bass. *Pugna certamen* and *Ah! troppo è ver* have concerto grosso instrumentation. In addition, *Alle selve, agli studii*, which is classed with the secular cantatas, is a *cantata morale* for four voices and basso continuo.

To sum up, *Esule dalle sfere* is an exceptional work for Stradella. A large work, it is one of the fifteen duets (according to Jander's classification); one of the five sacred cantatas, one of the two cantatas that employ a four-voice chorus, and one of the fourteen cantatas that have accompaniment other than continuo. It is further distinguished as one of the few cantatas for which the librettist is known.

Pompeo Figari and His Poems

Pompeo Figari was the librettist for *Esule dalle sfere*, according to the title page of the secondary manuscript source, Mus. F. 1148.[1] It is more difficult to sketch the biography of Figari than that of Stradella because even less information is available. In fact, practically all that is known about this minor seicento poet is found in writings of Giovanni Mario Crescimbeni (1663–1728), who chronicled the life of literary Italy around the turn of the seventeenth century. Birth and death dates are not available; the only dates that can be associated with Figari are those that connect him with a specific occurrence or a publication. The available information gives some idea of Figari's biographical data, his activity as a writer, his associations with the Roman Catholic church, and his reputation among his colleagues.

Crescimbeni reports that Figari returned to his native city of Genoa after living in Rome for a long time. He was one of the founders of the Arcadia,[2] a literary academy established in Rome on 5 October 1690. It was comprised of the followers of the literary circle of Queen Christina of Sweden, who died in 1689, and was dedicated to upholding the highest standards in Italian literature. Figari's name is recorded in activities of the Arcadia in Crescimbeni's history of Italian literature through 1697,[3] but he may have been still active in Rome in 1702, since he wrote the text to an oratorio that dates from that year. Figari's Arcadian name was Montano Falanzio, according to Crescimbeni's lists of members of the Arcadia.[4]

Figari has several literary works in Italian to his credit, but he apparently was not well known as a writer of Latin poetry.[5] Several of his poems are found in the Crescimbeni volumes,[6] and he is mentioned as being the poet for some songs.[7] Evidently his best-known work is a paraphrase of the seven penitential psalms, which are set as sonnets and entitled *Il salmista penitente*. Crescimbeni notes that Figari was making paraphrases of the Gradual psalms, also in sonnet form, when he returned to Genoa.[8] He wrote at least two works that he dedicated to a nephew of the pope. The first, entitled *L'Europa trionfante*, was a glorification of the sanctity of Pope Innocent XI and was dedicated to Signor D. Livio Odescalchi. It was published in Genoa in 1676. The second work, entitled *La contessa di Roma, e di Venezia*, was dedicated to Signor D. Pietro Ottoboni,[9] nephew of Pope Alexander VIII, who succeeded Pope Innocent XI in 1689. These *canzone*, as they were called, were published in Rome in that same year, when Pietro Ottoboni was made cardinal at the age of twenty-two. Figari's canzonetta about the "laughter and tears of Nigella" was singled out as a noteworthy example of the Arcadian Anacreontic canzonetta, a type of poetry reflecting amorous and convivial inter-

---

1. The manuscripts designated as "primary" and "secondary" sources for the present edition are described below on p. 29.

2. Crescimbeni, *L'istoria*, 2:542. The first edition (Rome, 1698), a one-volume work, also mentions Figari (p. 173). The sketch of his life is an abbreviated form of that in the third edition with the same poem presented to show his work but located in a separate place (p. 248).

3. Ibid., 6:228.

4. See ibid., 2:542, the main entry that includes a biographical sketch and a poem; also 6:401, 441; and Crescimbeni, *L'Arcadia*, pp. 16, 329.

5. Ademollo, *I teatri di Roma*, p. 186.

6. Crescimbeni, *L'istoria*, 1:218, 399; 2:542; *Le vite*, 2:248; *L'Arcadia*, pp. 117, 197, 310, 316.

7. Crescimbeni, *Le vite*, 2:288.

8. Crescimbeni, *L'istoria*, 2:542.

9. These two works are cataloged in Calvoli's *Biblioteca volante*, 2:318. According to Tiraboschi in *Storia della letteratura italiana* (vol. 8, pt. 1, pp. 429–31), Calvoli (1625–1706) was a medical doctor who was particularly interested in literature. A special project of his, *Biblioteca volante* was a catalog of small works he feared would escape the eye of even the most diligent scholar. These works were listed in the sixteen small volumes published by Calvoli and in material he left for four more volumes, which were alphabetized and published in four volumes by Dionigi Andrea Sancassani in 1734.

The second work mentioned above, *La contessa*, is a small twelve-page volume that is also listed in Piantanida, Diotallevi, and Livraghi, *Autori italiani del seicento*, 3:34.

ests.[10] The canzonetta is cited in *Rime d. avv. G. B. F. Zappi e di Faustina Maratti sua moglie* (Venice, 1736), a collection by contemporary poets that includes, in addition to poems by those named in the title, some by more celebrated members of the Arcadia.[11]

In addition to *Esule dalle sfere*, Figari wrote the text to another sacred cantata, *Crudo mar di fiamme orribili*, for which Stradella also composed the music. Figari wrote two oratorios, *Abram in Aegypto* (Rome, 1692) with music by Domenico Zazara[12] and *La conversione della Maddalena* (Rome, 1702) with music by Cinthio Vinchioni.[13] In his biography of Stradella, Remo Giazotto lists Figari as librettist for Stradella's opera, *Corispero*. Giazotto located the libretto in Genoa in the Biblioteca delle Missioni Urbane in a volume of miscellaneous sacred and secular works.[14] That library was bombed in World War II, however, and its few remaining works were scattered. No libretto is known to exist, nor is there a record of *Corispero*'s performance.[15] Figari also edited the works of other poets, a literary activity that has been documented. In 1697, when the Arcadians resolved to have a sixteenth-century poet's works reprinted with annotations, Figari was among those who applied themselves to this task.[16]

That Figari was a cleric may be concluded from several references to him as "Abate." On one occasion he is mentioned in connection with the Consistorial Congregation in Rome.[17] Indeed, many of his writings are religious, and both of the dedications mentioned above are to a nephew of the pope.

Figari's name is not prominent in literary sources, and he is clearly a minor figure. Yet as a founding father of the Arcadia, he moved in Rome's important literary circles. Crescimbeni reports that he did not wish to keep silent the "praised names of some of our Arcadians" and mentioned Figari's name first.[18] Figari was one of those many Italians during this time who possessed the ability to improvise in verse. In connection with this activity, he was a participant in an academy of improvisation that gathered around Cardinal Pietro Ottoboni,[19] the dedicatee of one of Figari's poem collections and a man who fostered a most extravagant patronage of the arts in Rome at the end of the seventeenth and beginning of the eighteenth centuries.[20] Figari was named in a poem by Girolamo Baruffaldi as one of "three rare talents from Liguria," the region of Italy in which Figari's native Genoa is located.[21] Additional evidence of Figari's reputation is seen by his "introduction under the name of Alindo into the Congressi Letterarj of the most erudite Norcia."[22] Finally, the appearance of Figari's name on *Esule dalle sfere* may further attest to his prominence since most of Stradella's librettists are unknown and those named are relatively well-known Italian poets: Giovanni Pietro Monesio, Nicolò Minato, Francesco Maria Sereni, and Sebastiano Baldini, for example.[23]

The intriguing question is when, or if, Figari and Stradella collaborated on *Esule dalle sfere*. They clearly moved in the same circles, though not necessarily at the same time, for some of the members of the Arcadia were Stradella's patrons when he was in

---

10. Natali, *Storia letteraria d'italia*, 2:674.
11. Ibid., pp. 760–61.
12. Ademollo, *I teatri di Roma*, p. 186.
13. Smither, *Oratorio*, 1:304.
14. Giazotto, *Vita*, 2:813.
15. Gianturco, "Operas," p. 90.
16. Crescimbeni, *L'istoria*, 6:228.
17. Crescimbeni, *Le vite*, 2:286. This congregation was an assembly of cardinals called by the pope for consultation on matters of grave importance.
18. Ibid., 1:157.
19. Crescimbeni, *L'istoria*, 1:220–21; *L'Arcadia*, pp. 116–20.
20. See Marx, "Musik am Hofe Ottobonis unter Corelli."
21. Natali, *Storia letteraria d'italia*, 2:667–68. Baruffaldi (1675–1755), a Ferrarese and high priest of Cento, has several literary works to his credit, including *Tabaccheide* (Ferrara, 1714), the collection in which this poem appears. Baruffaldi may have become acquainted with Figari's work through Arcadian connections since, under the name Cluento Nettunio, he was a member of the Ferrarese colony of the Arcadia (Crescimbeni, *L'istoria*, 6:242, 373, 421, 436). That a Ferrarese, who was high priest of Cento (located between Bologna and Ferrara), should name Figari as one of the rare talents of Ligura indicates that his fame was more than local.
22. Crescimbeni, *L'istoria*, 2:542. Natali (*Storia letteraria d'italia*, 2:1186) refers to the work by Antonio Domenico Norcia, *I congressi letterarii* (Florence, 1707). Crescimbeni reports that Norcia, a Florentine, was also a member of the Arcadia under the name Gomero Aloneo (*L'istoria*, 4:254; 6:447). When the third edition of *L'istoria* was published, a list of members indicated Norcia was canon of S. Lorenzo in Damaso (6:391); he also lived in Rome at one time. *I congressi letterarii* is mentioned in the biographical sketch that accompanies the main entry for Norcia.
23. In one final reference to Figari, Natali (*Storia letteraria d'italia*, 2:761) reports that there are four articles on Figari by Arturo Ferretto, an official of the Archivio di Stato in Genoa, in the periodical *Il mare* (27 April to 20 July 1912) of Rapallo, a seacoast town to the south of Genoa and a favorite residence for literati, artists, and musicians.

Rome. Based on known facts (the date on the secondary source is 1680;[24] a reference to Figari associated with Genoa is dated 1676;[25] Stradella was in Genoa some time after 10 October 1677; all references to Figari associated with Rome are after 1689),[26] at least three possibilities exist, none of them definitive: (1) Stradella may have collaborated with Figari in Genoa some time after 10 October 1677 before Figari went to Rome; (2) Stradella may have written the cantata in Rome before 1677 and Figari could already have been there; (3) Stradella could have acquired Figari's poem and may have written the music in Rome before 1677 or in Genoa after 1677 without direct collaboration with Figari. In the last two possibilities, the date on the secondary source need not be the date of composition. The paper and scribe of the principal source (an undated copy, not an autograph) have been identified as Roman,[27] thus lending support to Rome as a place of composition. However, Genoa seems just as strong a contender because Stradella was there some time after 10 October 1677 and Figari as late as 1676 (and not in Rome until about 1689) and because the cantata is obviously a mature work.

---

24. This is also the date that appears on the edition of the independent four-movement sinfonia published by Silvani in Bologna. See the discussion of sources on pp. 00–00.

25. This was *L'Europa trionfante* (Genoa, 1676).

26. This was *La contessa di Roma* (Rome, 1689).

27. Jander, *Alessandro Stradella*, WECIS fasc. 4a, no. 160.

The Work in Historical Context: Cantata and Oratorio

One of the puzzling questions about *Esule dalle sfere* is how it relates to the music genres of seventeenth-century Italy. *Esule dalle sfere* is designated a *cantata* in its two sources. Yet its forces are relatively large: two soloists, a chorus with two solo roles, and a basso continuo instrumental accompaniment joined by two violins for certain sections. A performance of the work lasts some thirty-five to forty minutes. Its libretto tells of souls tormented by Lucifero and of the intervention of Angelo, who takes them to Paradise.

The seicento has long been known for its ambiguity of terminology with respect to music genres of the time—cantata, opera, oratorio, serenata, intermezzo, and numerous others. Two terms are of particular importance with respect to *Esule dalle sfere*: *cantata*, the label in its sources, and *oratorio*, a genre that it resembles. A brief sketch of the history of these two genres may clarify its relationship to each.

This investigation is limited primarily to Rome for several reasons. First, although the date of *Esule dalle sfere* suggests its composition in Genoa, the environs of Rome had been Stradella's home for several years and had greatly influenced him. Second, the flowering of both the cantata and oratorio took place in Rome around the middle of the seventeenth century. Third, much of the scholarly work that has been done up to now concerns Rome.

A thoroughgoing treatment of the cantata, such as the opera, oratorio, and sonata have received,[1] is lacking at this time. Although pioneering studies have added a great deal to our understanding of the cantata,[2] they are now dated; their conclusions were based on a limited amount of information gained a number of years ago. Several excellent studies of the cantatas of individual composers have been made more recently,[3] but many others are needed. The Wellesley Edition Cantata Index Series (WECIS) indexes numerous cantatas from the seventeenth century,[4] but it is by no means complete. Although an excellent short survey of the Italian cantata in the Baroque was made by Gloria Rose in 1967[5] and another appears in the *New Grove* by Nigel Fortune, Colin Timms, and Malcolm Boyd,[6] the completion of a more extensive general history of the cantata is eagerly awaited.[7]

As far as is known, the term *cantata* was first used to designate a piece of music in the *Cantade et arie a voce sola* by Alessandro Grandi, which was reprinted

---

1. In addition to numerous specialized studies of these genres, each has been the subject of the following general works: Grout, *A Short History of Opera*; Smither, *A History of the Oratorio*; Newman, *A History of the Sonata Idea*.

2. The most thorough study of the cantata was made by Schmitz, *Geschichte der Kantate*. Other early studies include Dent, "Italian Chamber Cantatas"; and Prunières, "The Italian Cantata of the XVII Century."

3. Among the recent studies of cantatas of individual composers are the following Ph.D. dissertations: Rose, "The Cantatas of Carissimi"; Burrows, "The Cantatas of Antonio Cesti"; Eisley, "The Secular Cantatas of Mario Savioni"; Hanley, "Alessandro Scarlatti's *Cantate da camera*"; the dissertation by Caluori was revised and published as *The Cantatas of Luigi Rossi*. In addition, there are dissertations that deal with specific aspects of composers' cantatas. See also the article by Rose, "The Cantatas of Giacomo Carissimi."

4. To date, seven fascicles have been issued: 1, *Antonio Cesti* (comp. David L. Burrows); 2, *Mario Savioni* (comp. Irving R. Eisley); 3, *Luigi Rossi* (comp. Eleanor Caluori, also published by UMI Research Press); *Alessandro Stradella* (comp. Owen Jander); 5, *Giacomo Carissimi* (comp. Gloria Rose); and 8/9, *Alessandro and Atto Melani* (comp. Robert L. Weaver). In addition, the Scarlatti study by Hanley contains an exhaustive thematic catalog and index.

5. Rose, "Italian Cantata."

6. *New Grove*, 3:694–702, s.v. "Cantata."

7. At the present time Colin Timms and John Wendham of the Barber Institute of Fine Arts at the University of Birmingham are collaborating on a book entitled "The Italian Cantata, 1600–1725," to be published by Cambridge University Press. They plan to outline the main features of the cantata and its history by organizing the material around key composers, patrons, poets, and centers. Attention will be paid to the texts of the cantatas in relation to seventeenth-century Italian poetry in general. The authors also plan to include a bibliography of modern editions in their book.

in Venice in 1620 (the original publication date is unknown). The term was used irregularly throughout the first part of the century by such lesser known composers as Carlo Milanuzzi (1624), Giovanni Pietro Berti (1624 and 1627), Francesco Turini (1624), Domenico Crivellati (1628), Giovanni Rovetta (1629 and 1640), Giovanni Felice Sances (1633 and 1636), Francesco Negri (1635), Martino Pesenti (1636), and Rinieri Scarselli (1642).[8] Not until the 1670s did the term begin to be used in the sources with increasing frequency,[9] and in musical sources closest to Stradella the term is not often found.[10]

Although Grandi seems to have been the first to use the term, numerous scholars of this century have named earlier compositions *cantatas* by virtue of their style and structure. For example, Gustave Reese cites Giaches de Wert's *L'ottavo libro de madrigali* (1586) as "virtually secular cantatas in madrigalian form."[11] Alfred Einstein speaks of the last six madrigals of Monteverdi's *Il quinto libro de madrigali* (1606) as being related to the cantata. He calls the final number "a real *concento*, a real concerto, a real cantata, with an overture (*Sinfonia*) and a ritornello."[12] Actually, a cursory examination of the music from the first part of the seventeenth century indicates that the terminology of the period was not entirely indiscriminate.[13]

Theorists and historians in the seicento were silent as to the definition of the term *cantata*. The few treatises that discuss secular music at all employ nearly as many terms as there are musical sources. Angelo Berardi is the one theorist who mentions the cantata. In his *Ragionamenti musicali* (1681), he says that the cantata is one of three styles for the chamber.[14] In *L'istoria della volgar poesia* (1698), Giovanni Mario Crescimbeni considers the cantata a recognized poetical form and further comments that it thoroughly deserves its great popularity.[15] The earliest definition of the cantata as a music genre is found in Sébastien de Brossard's monumental *Dictionaire de musique* (1703).[16]

Modern definitions of the cantata are similar. Eugen Schmitz, who wrote one of the early studies of the cantata, defined the secular solo cantata in mid-century as a vocal piece for one voice with accompaniment, a piece with a structure made up of individual sections that contrasted in some manner (meter or tempo changes, alternation of recitative and aria, changes in types of dramatic expression).[17] However, in broadening Schmitz's definition, sources today agree that the cantata in seventeenth-century Italy was usually a secular composition for solo voice (but perhaps for two or three voices), with basso continuo accompaniment and an Italian poetic text. Whereas the cantata took many forms during its history, its true nature was governed by its function as chamber music, music to be performed by skilled musicians for an audience of knowledgeable listeners.[18]

Numerous problems arise in naming works from the first half of the century *cantata*. Not only have scholars referred to early compositions as *cantatas* because they were similar to later works bearing that name, but they also have not made entirely clear the distinction between *cantata* and other names that circulated. It is well known now that the roots of the cantata are in monody—solo song with basso continuo accompaniment. In fact, as Rose has stated, "Monody and cantata are essentially the same thing at different stages of development."[19] Therefore, if one wishes to undertake a comprehensive survey of the cantata throughout the century, one must begin with an investigation of monody.

By the end of the sixteenth century, the style of the madrigal was changing. Its polyphonic texture was being replaced by a more harmonically conceived

---

8. Schmitz, *Geschichte der Kantate*, pp. 25, 68–69; early usage of the term is described briefly by Colin Timms in the *New Grove*, 3:695, s.v. "Cantata."
9. Rose, "Italian Cantata," p. 670.
10. Jander, *Alessandro Stradella*, WECIS fasc. 4a, p. 3.
11. Reese, *Music in the Renaissance*, p. 409.
12. Einstein, *Italian Madrigal*, 2:854.
13. Rose, "Italian Cantata," p. 658.
14. According to Rose, "Cantatas of Carissimi" (dissertation), p. 23.
15. Crescimbeni, *L'istoria*, 1:299–300.

16. According to Rose, "Cantatas of Carissimi" (dissertation), p. 24. An English translation of the Brossard definition (s.v. "Cantata") reads as follows: "CANTATA, pl. Cantate.... It is a large piece, the words of which are in Italian, with a variety of recitatives, ariettas, and different movements; usually for solo voice and basso continuo, often with two violins or several instruments, etc. When the words concern piety or morality, they are called *cantate morali ò spirituali*; when they speak of love, they are *cantate amoresè*, etc."
17. Schmitz, *Geschichte der Kantate*, pp. 66–67.
18. Rose, "Italian Cantata," p. 655.
19. Ibid., p. 656.

style that often involved contrasts in dramatic expression, an increasingly important upper voice, a bass voice acting as a foundation, and an emphasis on virtuosity. Opera and solo song were also growing in importance, with solo song reaching a far wider public than opera.[20] After Giulio Caccini published *Le nuove musiche* (Florence, 1601/2), many composers throughout Italy began to imitate his new style and to publish their works in collections of some twenty to thirty songs. The new style then became widely known in Italy through these collections, which included some dialogues and duets.[21]

Early monody flourished in three cities: Florence, Venice, and Rome. In Florence, where it first developed, the main activity occurred before 1620 and died without founding a tradition. Venice was the city where most monodies were published, though at first very few were composed there.[22] Rome saw much activity from the beginning, for the first collection of monodies was published there in 1608.[23] Yet the first Roman monodies, which were sacred, did not approach the splendor of the Florentine works.[24] Because of the generous support given to the arts in Rome, however, the city lured a number of eminent professional musicians who would change the picture by mid-century.

Roman society attracted these musicians and in turn supported monody and the cantata, the chamber music of the socially elite.[25] This Roman milieu was unique in that the church and the higher circles of society were inextricably linked. To a large extent, the atmosphere in Rome depended on the sentiments of the pope toward the arts. Of the popes through Stradella's time, Urban VIII (Maffeo Barberini, 1623–44) was an ardent patron of the arts; during his tenure numerous artists and musicians were drawn to the city. The next pope to take an interest in the arts was Alexander VII (Fabio Chigi, 1655–67), who is known for his reform of liturgical music. Also favorably disposed to music, literature, and art was Clement IX (Giulio Rospigliosi, 1667–69), who had been the librettist for a number of operas. On the other hand, Innocent XI (Benedetto Odescalchi, 1676–89) initiated policies hostile to the theater, policies that led to Stradella's departure from Rome in 1677. Other patrons of the arts included the Barberini, Pamphilj, Colonna, and Chigi families, and Queen Christina of Sweden, who, after abdicating her throne and converting to Catholicism, lived in Rome from 1656 until her death in 1689. Occasions for performances were numerous. Patrons as private individuals and as members of institutions employed musicians in their households, sponsored private concerts, and commissioned works for certain celebrations. In addition, there were meetings of religious organizations and academies, ecclesiastical festivals, theological debates, and various ceremonies such as those for the presentation of doctorates. By mid-century the published literature that had been so important for monody diminished in favor of manuscript collections, perhaps for economic reasons. Cantatas had become so popular and so numerous that they dominated the field of vocal chamber music. No one edition could hope to capture the market and show profit. In Rome especially, the number of manuscripts far outweighed the printed sources,[26] presumably because patrons tended to think of both the music and the manuscript as private creations. Extant manuscripts, many of them anthologies, are sometimes quite elegant.

An examination of the texts reveals that most of them were written by dilettantes, many of them friends of the composers. Aristocrats, ecclesiastics, and sometimes the composers themselves were included as poets. These amateurs, usually unnamed, often modeled their verses after the highly stylized language of Giambattista Marino (1569–1625), whose influence extended throughout the century. The language of these cantata verses, typical of the seventeenth century, expressed the simplest thought in a most complicated manner by means of surprising similes, metaphors, and other rhetorical devices. Since poets were concerned with the sound of the

---

20. Fortune, "Italian Secular Monody," pp. 171–72. See also Fortune's more recent article, "Monody," in the *New Grove*, 12:497–98.
21. See the recent study by John Whenham, "Italian Secular Duets and Dialogues."
22. Fortune, "Italian Secular Monody," pp. 186–89.
23. For a thorough treatment of the early monody and cantata in Rome, see Rose, "Cantatas of Carissimi" (dissertation), pp. 32–49.
24. Fortune, "Italian Secular Monody," p. 186.
25. For an excellent description of patronage in Rome, see Haskell, *Patrons and Painters*, especially for the first half of the seicento; for the last third of the century, see Bridges, "Social Setting of *Musica da camera* in Rome."

26. Rose, "Italian Cantata," p. 660.

language, they frequently used verbal play, alliteration, and assonance. Love, especially unrequited love, was their favorite topic, the pastoral scene a popular setting. However, they also turned to nonamorous topics of a moral or spiritual nature. Records from Rome around Stradella's time suggest that this nonamorous type—allegorical, mythological, or religious—was often used for the serious meetings and ceremonies mentioned above.[27]

Since most composers of the time wrote at least some cantatas, a list of cantata composers in Rome would include the most important composers during the mid-century period. These included Luigi Rossi, Giacomo Carissimi, Pietro Simone Agostini, Carlo Caproli, Antonio Cesti, Marco Marazzoli, Giovanni Marciani, Domenico and Virgilio Mazzocchi, Atto Melani, Orazio Michi, Bernardo Pasquini, Marc'-Antonio Pasqualini, Mario Savioni, Alessandro Stradella, and Antonio Francesco Tenaglia. Toward the end of the century, Alessandro Scarlatti was the most important cantata composer who had Roman connections—he began his distinguished career in Rome.

The characteristics of the music in cantatas are difficult to trace because manuscripts containing cantatas generally were not dated. Differences in the style of cantatas in Rome as well as throughout Italy apparently depended on individual composers. Therefore, in order to encompass the stylistic variety of cantatas written by numerous composers, any description of the early cantata must remain broad. The most recent scholarship on the cantata identifies two general types up to the 1670s: works consisting of a single aria (*ariette corte*) and works in several sections (*arie di più parte*). In the multisectional type, an individual section could be in recitative, arioso, or aria style, or a combination of these, depending on the text.[28]

There is evidence that the term *cantata* took on a more uniform meaning during the decade after 1670, when it began to be found more frequently on sources. By this time, the majority of cantatas were extended compositions with contrasting sections. The major change in the cantata around the 1670s entailed an increase in size and variety; the contrasting sections within each cantata became longer, as did the work itself. Recitatives and arias became more clearly delineated, and sometimes other instruments were used in addition to the continuo. Examination of cantatas reveals that some were in binary and ternary design, some were strophic, others employed the rondo in some way, and still others were composite or through-composed. Various combinations of these designs were also employed. Not until the beginning of the eighteenth century did the cantatas of the most prolific composer, Scarlatti, crystallize into the typical scheme of two contrasting arias, one or both preceded by a recitative.[29]

Although most of the works designated *cantata* are solo works accompanied only by basso continuo, a few large works also bear this name.[30] Some of the works with allegorical or mythological subjects were large cantatas, perhaps with choruses. Gloria Rose, who cataloged Carissimi's cantatas, considers the three-voice cantatas actually secular counterparts of his oratorios.[31] In his study of Scarlatti's chamber cantatas, Edwin Hanley does not even list the large cantatas, since they were designed not for chamber but for official court functions or important occasions often celebrated in connection with operatic performances. Usually longer than *cantate da camera*, these larger works required two to five singers, perhaps a chorus, and frequently extensive instrumental forces. These works are usually labeled *serenata*, but some are labeled *cantata*. Hanley further observes that the terms *cantata* or *cantata spirituale* are sometimes used in Scarlatti's works to designate an *oratorio*.[32] An interesting mixture of terms surrounds some of Savioni's large works. In the preface to his *Concerti morali e spirituali* (1660), an important collection in the development of the multivoice cantata,[33]

---

27. For a description of these works, see Bridges, "Social Setting of *Musica da camera* in Rome," pp. 68–99, 165–66.

28. See the discussion by Colin Timms in the *New Grove*, 3:695, s.v. "Cantata."

29. Hanley, "Scarlatti's *Cantate da camera*," p. 70.

30. In the Biblioteca Estense at Modena, there is a small group of cantatas bearing captions such as *cantata in accademia*, or a similar title including the word *accademia*. These works were composed in the 1680s for the Accademia de' Dissonante, and, like serenatas, were large-scale occasional cantatas. Possibly the same type of composition was written in Rome about the same time for the academies. See Jander, "The *Cantata in accademia*."

31. Rose, "Cantatas of Carissimi" (dissertation), p. 118. Sartori's *Carissimi: Catalogo delle opere attribuite* does not list the works according to number of voices.

32. Hanley, "Scarlatti's *Cantate da camera*," pp. 63–66.

33. Eisley, "Cantatas of Savioni," p. 56.

Savioni states that if singers are pleased with these pieces, he promises to follow them with "a group of madrigals for five voices, likewise moral, which will serve to be sung at the end of each concerto [of this book] . . . thus cantatas for oratories will be completed."[34] It is interesting to note that this description of a complete cantata for an oratory fits Savioni's only known composition that is labeled *oratorio* in its source.[35]

Thus, ambiguity of terminology existed with regard to these larger works, and the term that may reasonably be associated with them today, in particular the sacred ones, is *oratorio*. *Esule dalle sfere*, one of these larger cantatas with a sacred text, is similar to the oratorio, a genre that will now be examined.

The oratorio is nearly always a sacred, unstaged work with a dramatic or narrative-dramatic text. Some differences in concept exist from one subperiod of the Baroque to another and to some extent from one geographical area to another, according to Howard E. Smither, who based this conclusion on writings about Baroque music and on his study of the primary sources of compositions called *oratorios*.[36]

An understanding of the early oratorio depends in part on an understanding of its social context. The same society that nurtured the cantata also supported the oratorio. Of particular importance to the oratorio, however, was the immediate social context within which it originated, that is, the religious communities that held prayer services in buildings called *oratories*. The Congregation of the Oratory was founded by St. Philip Neri in the second half of the sixteenth century with the idea of attracting all types of people in order to lead them on a path to salvation.[37] The idea of Neri's congregation soon began to spread, and numerous similar congregations were started, first in Rome and then throughout Italy. The meeting place of each group was often the oratory (*oratorio* in Italian), a small hall adjacent to the main church building. By the 1640s, the word *oratorio* was used for some musical works performed there. Later in the century, the concept of the oratorio became more that of a concert work than a vehicle for devotion; indeed, the oratorio became a composition approaching opera in style and function. Educational institutions, private palaces of patrons, and on a very special occasion (Christmas Eve) the Vatican Apostolic Palace served as places for performances in addition to oratories.[38] Oratorios were often substituted for operas, especially during the Lenten season when opera theaters were closed; and performances of oratorios, like those of cantatas, were sponsored by private patrons.

Likewise, the texts of oratorios changed somewhat during the course of the century. The earliest works for the oratory fit the highly contemplative service modeled after the personality of Neri, its founder. Popular subjects included laments of Mary Magdalene as well as laments of the Virgin Mary at the Crucifixion of Jesus.[39] By 1660 the texts, reflective or dramatic, were simple and intended to appeal to a wide audience. In the dramatic type of oratorio, the narrative element was presented by a *testo*, or narrator. The text generally came from the Old or New Testament, hagiography, or other sources of spiritual and moral topics.[40] During the last half century in particular, Christian virtues were allegorically presented. Most texts of the later period featured a strong conflict between good and evil or between heaven and the world.[41]

Immediate antecedents of the oratorio include the late Renaissance gospel motets and laude, early operas, dramatic dialogues, and brief secular cantatas for one or more solo voices. In addition, a few cantatas had spiritual texts musically similar to the secular cantata, although they were more closely related to the oratorio as a distinct music genre.[42] Thus, the oratorio emerged as a result of the complex interaction of social and musical influences during the seventeenth century. Two basic types appeared that differed from a literary standpoint, though not from a musical one: the *oratorio volgare*, which employed an Italian text, usually in poetry; and the *oratorio latino*, which used a Latin text, predominantly in prose.[43] The first type was more closely associated with the cantata.

---

34. The quotation from the preface of Savioni's *Concerti*, p. 5, is given in Smither, *Oratorio*, 1:165.
35. Ibid., p. 166.
36. Ibid., pp. 3–4.
37. Ibid., p. 9.
38. Ibid., p. 275.
39. Ibid., p. 164.
40. Ibid., pp. 204–5.
41. Ibid., pp. 299–303.
42. Ibid., p. 12.
43. Ibid., p. 207.

Little is known about the music during the formative period (before ca. 1640) of the *oratorio volgare*, when the terminology was so ambiguous. Extant records in the earliest oratories do not go into detail, but undoubtedly dialogues were sometimes used. As was noted in the preface of the Savioni *Concerti*, the oratorio was closely associated with the cantata and the madrigal. The one-movement compositions similar to those of Savioni that were used in oratorios appear under a variety of names, including *oratorio*, *cantata*, *concerto*, and *dialogo*. The latter three terms might be modified by the adjective *morale* or *spirituale*, or might be combined with some additional term that indicates the work was for an oratory. There were also two-part compositions called *oratories* that employed the terms *prima cantata* and *seconda cantata* for the two parts. In performance a one-part composition came before the sermon and another followed the sermon; or a two-part composition was divided and performed before and after the sermon.[44] By mid-century, oratorios comprised one part with a duration of twenty to thirty minutes or two parts with a duration of forty-five minutes to an hour.

Within these works there is usually one singer per character, and choruses and ensembles represent groups of characters and crowds. Such works typically close with a moralizing chorus; in fact, many use the chorus only at the end of a work or at the end of each part of a two-part work. The style of writing for the solo parts is typical of writing for the cantata and opera of the period in that recitative, arioso, and aria are blended together. Also the same numerous aria forms found in the cantata are employed. Choral ensemble music is both chordal and imitative, with the vocal lines not difficult in most works. If instruments other than those for continuo are used, they are usually two violins. Instruments play the introduction, support the chorus, play the ritornellos occurring throughout, and occasionally accompany a solo voice.[45]

From the 1660s to about 1720, the oratorio changed considerably. Since its function changed from a means of attracting a crowd into an oratory for a spiritual exercise to an entertainment for its own sake, both the libretto and the music more closely approached opera. Consequently, an increasing number of theatrical effects were incorporated in oratorios. As in the earlier period, many other terms were applied to the oratorio, and again one of them was *cantata*. One use of the term was for the special oratoriolike work that was performed on Christmas Eve at the Apostolic Palace. This reflective cantata of praise was prominent in the 1670s and 1680s.[46] In fact, Stradella composed two cantatas for Christmas Eve, at least one of which may have been performed at this time.[47]

In this later period, oratorios tended to have two parts that lasted a total of one and one-half to two hours. Earlier works, including those by Stradella, were shorter. Usually three to five characters were employed. The chorus, an ensemble of the soloists, was rarely used in the oratorios of the late seventeenth to early eighteenth centuries, and the requirement of a separate choral group was rare after Carissimi.[48] The music after about 1660 was still a free mingling of passages in recitative, arioso, and aria. From the 1680s on, however, a regular alternation of recitative and aria was characteristic. Arias, which tended to become longer as the century progressed, were still cast in a variety of forms. The da capo form in oratorio dates from about the last decade of the century. Some oratorios call for two or three strings in addition to the basso continuo; after about 1680 more varied orchestras were employed, including the concerto grosso instrumentation found in Stradella's Roman works as early as the 1660s. The instrumental groups played an increasingly important role both in the amount of vocal material they accompanied and in the length of the purely instrumental sections. There was a progressive tendency toward orchestral accompaniment of the aria, whereas the basso continuo still accompanied recitative.[49]

---

44. Ibid., pp. 164–67.
45. Ibid., pp. 204–6.
46. Ibid., p. 275.
47. These two works are *Ah! troppo è ver*, in I/Tn: Giordano 12, fols. 1–64, and I/MOe: Mus. F. 1145; and *Si apra al riso ogni labbro*, in I/MOe: Mus. F. 1144. The former is an elaborate work scored for six solo voices, chorus, and concerto grosso instrumentation; the latter, smaller in scope, is for soprano, alto, bass, two violins, and continuo, and seems to be an early work.
48. Smither, *Oratorio*, 1:297–99, 306.
49. Ibid., pp. 306–8, 333–35, 361–62. For a discussion of Stradella's use of concerto grosso in Roman works, see Jander, "Concerto Grosso Instrumentation in Rome"; see also Franco Piperno, "Le viole divise in due cori: poli cora lità e 'concerto' nella

A look at the names of composers prominent in the composition of oratorios in the mid-century period reveals that some of them were also prominent in the field of cantata and opera: Domenico Mazzocchi, Pietro Della Valle, Francesco Balducci, Marco Marazzoli, and Giacomo Carissimi. From the 1660s to the 1680s, Giovanni Legrenzi, Stradella,[50] and Giovanni Paolo Colonna were among the most important figures; from the 1680s to about 1720, the most significant composers included Scarlatti, Handel, Vivaldi, and Caldara.[51]

How does *Esule dalle sfere* relate to the cantata and oratorio of the seicento? It is reasonable to call the work a *cantata*, because it is so designated in its sources and because it shares characteristics with the cantata—the stylized language of the text, the intermingling of sacred and secular elements, and the flexible style of the music, with varying sections that merge into one another. Yet this is an exceptional cantata: it includes a chorus, more than one solo voice plus violins, and a sacred text.

On the other hand, it also would seem appropriate to call the work an oratorio. It is almost as long as the one-section oratorios of the time. The number of voices or groups of voices corresponds to the number of characters or groups of characters in the text (three or five, depending on whether the two members of the chorus having solo parts are counted individually). The text, like those of oratorios, consists entirely of dramatic dialogue with some of the characters' speeches incorporating reflective elements. *Esule dalle sfere* resembles some earlier oratorios in its use of a chorus, but differs from the later oratorios, which tend to use an ensemble of the soloists as the chorus. Unlike the usual oratorio of its time, however, this work does not employ a *testo*. The flexible style of its music is a characteristic feature of both cantata and oratorio.

For this work, then, the terms *dramatic cantata* and *oratorio* would seem to be equally appropriate and indeed interchangeable. Seicento terms need not be considered mutually exclusive and they were not so considered at the time. Thus viewed in its historical context, *Esule dalle sfere* is both a cantata and an oratorio.

---

musica di Alessandro Stradella," in *Atti del convegno internationale Alessandro Stradella: Siena 1982*, a volume of *Chigiana*, currently in press.

50. Stradella wrote seven oratorios, six of which are extant. For a discussion of them, see Smither, *Oratorio*, 1:314–26, and Gianturco, "Oratorios." For an extensive discussion and edition of *San Giovanni Battista*, see Daniels, "San Giovanni Battista."

51. The composers named were the ones treated most extensively by Smither.

Structure and Style

An examination of *Esule dalle sfere* reveals certain distinguishing characteristics of structure and style. A brief overview of the characters, text, and music will be followed by a description of the structure and style of the various sections: recitatives, arias, choruses, and instrumental sections. One fascinating feature clearly stands out: Stradella was a master at conveying through music the meaning of the text at all levels—the overall meaning of the text as a whole, the thought within each section, and the meaning of specific words.

The cantata includes two characters, Lucifero and Angelo, and a four-voice chorus of souls in Purgatory, of which the soprano and bass have solo roles.[1] Lucifero, a bass, has some of the *basso buffo* traits of the next century. He tends to be dramatic, especially at first, and at times is even somewhat comic. Angelo is characterized as a beautiful, helpful being. The tormented souls express their suffering in their chorus and solo parts; a heavy gloom and darkness seem to surround them.

The text begins with Lucifero seeking revenge on the souls in Purgatory before they ascend to Heaven. The souls plead for help; they hope for the day when their suffering will end and they can go to Heaven. Suddenly Angelo appears and orders Lucifero to stop the torture. He tells the souls to be merry and fly with him to Heaven; through the power of the prayers of mortals, they now have wings to fly to Heaven. He tells Lucifero that the souls are not actually wicked. Giving up, Lucifero goes back to his home, and the souls fly with Angelo to Paradise. Like some oratorio librettos of the period, this one is essentially dramatic and includes conflict between the forces of God and Lucifer. The text is not specifically from the Bible but deals with an apocryphal subject. The text, predominantly in verse, determines the type of music that is used.

The music is basically through-composed, but there is some repetition of phrases and sections. Beginning with a two-movement introductory sinfonia, the cantata is a composite of choral sections and solos in recitative, arioso, and aria styles, with an occasional instrumental ritornello interspersed. At times the soloists sing in rapid succession, but never do they interrupt each other. Although the nonformalized sections tend to merge, some sections are self-contained, namely, the arias and the choral and instrumental sections. With the exception of three a cappella choruses (four in the secondary manuscript copy), the cantata is accompanied by basso continuo. Two violins join the continuo for Angelo's two arias, the soprano Anima's aria, all but the middle section of Lucifero's arias, the final choral section, and the instrumental sinfonia and ritornellos.

Recitatives

The recitatives in *Esule dalle sfere* tend to be short and syllabic, but occasionally Lucifero's recitative is melismatic. The continuo line of recitatives usually begins with a long-held note over which the harmony may change. As the recitative progresses, the bass line motion increases and the writing takes on features of arioso style. Sometimes the style even approaches that of the aria, as in one of Lucifero's recitatives (no. 2).[2] After an important cadence is reached within the recitative, it is typical for increased motion in the bass line to begin again.

Several unusual places in the recitatives may be noted. Lucifero's first recitative (no. 2) is particularly well developed. Much longer than other recitatives in the cantata, it contains remarkable melismas that make demands on the singer, repeats phrases for emphasis, and is highly dramatic. Its last phrase, which has a long melisma, is repeated with an even

---

1. The bass part is in the secondary manuscript source only.

2. Numbers in parentheses refer to corresponding sections in the score.

longer one, a formal procedure used by many composers of later generations especially.

The bass Anima's recitative (no. 11a) is unusual in that the type of writing employed, especially at the end, is reminiscent of older techniques with its short sections and changes of meter at the beginning of each. The text—"Sù, sù, crescete, accendete, abbruciate, saziatevi al fin. Ma poi cessate"—is repeated. At the phrase "Sù . . . al fin" ("Up, up, grow, flare up, burn, satisfy yourselves at last"), the tempo is marked *presto* for six measures. Then, for the three measures with "Ma poi cessate" ("But then, cease"), the tempo designation changes to *adagio*, and the music, illustrating these words, slowly ceases. As the text is repeated, so is the tempo sequence. This recitative has the only tempo marks in the entire cantata, and only here does such sectional writing occur within a unit.

Arias

There are five arias in *Esule dalle sfere*: two for Angelo (nos. 22, 26) and one each for the soprano Anima (no. 8), the bass Anima (no. 11b), and Lucifero (nos. 3–4). The arias are self-contained units with clear formal structures. More so than in other sections, the tonality tends to be clearer, key centers are more closely related, and many of the chord roots progress by fifths. Melodies in the soprano arias, especially Angelo's, may be described as bel canto, whereas the bass arias have more angular melodic lines.

Lucifero's aria is of particular interest. Although it appears on the manuscript page as if it were two separate sections, a closer examination reveals a mature da capo aria of some dimension (no. 3–A and no. 4–BA). The first section (no. 3–A) has sixty-three measures in 3/8 meter on the text "Mie schiere severe, vendetta! Sù, sù!" Framed by a ritornello, this section has an introductory phrase that is repeated, has the inner form aba', and moves harmonically from D major to A major, then back to D major. The beginning of the second section (no. 4–B of BA) provides contrast in that the meter changes to C, the continuo employs an ostinato figure, and the violins are omitted. Unlike the A section that is framed by a ritornello, the B section is introduced by the one-measure ostinato figure. However, like the A section, the initial phrase of B is repeated. The keys employed are D major, G major, and A major. The last note of this twenty-six measure B section occurs in the first measure where the meter changes back to 3/8; thus, the ostinato section has merged into a written-out repetition of the first section (A), which is exact except for an exchange of violin parts in the opening ritornello. If we consider the well-developed recitative that precedes this aria, we find a recitative with da capo aria much like those of the eighteenth century. This unit, which conveys Lucifero's vow to torture the souls before they go to Heaven and his inciting of his hordes to revenge, shows him in complete control, flaunting his glory.

The bass Anima's aria, "Crude voragini" (no. 11b), is likewise a dramatic aria with melismas. Unlike Lucifero's aria, this one is accompanied by continuo only. A unique characteristic of this aria is its ostinato bass, which is prominent throughout the last part. The bass Anima's recitative-aria unit (missing in the primary source) occurs at a place in the cantata where the souls are in the depths of despair with no hope in sight. Stradella's dramatic treatment of the text at this point is highly effective.

Angelo's aria, "Sù, sù, spariscano" (no. 22), is one of the most attractive sections of the cantata. Its ABA design is that of the da capo aria except that it is less developed than the mature arias in the next century or even Lucifero's aria discussed above. For example, like many mature da capo arias, contrast between the A and B sections is created by a change in time signature from 3/4 to C and a change in the style of writing. However, unlike many mature da capo arias, the texts of the two sections are not contrasting nor are the A and B sections well developed tonally. Reflective in nature, the music pictures the angel who hastens the torments away, then invites the souls to fly with him to Heaven. The other two arias, Angelo's "A cor supplicante" (no. 26) and Anima's "Troppo avari" (no. 8), both reflective, are also in ABA' design and are even less fully developed than "Sù, sù, spariscano."

In both recitatives and arias, Stradella uses musical figures effectively. For example, at the end of Lucifero's recitative (no. 2, mm. 27ff., 33ff.), one notes the long melismas on "portino" as Lucifero declares that the souls being purged should *carry* the marks of his revenge. In his aria (no. 4, mm. 18, 20), it is interesting to observe the melismas on "l'ali" when he mentions what will happen to the souls "before they *wing* their way to Heaven." "Inferno" receives special attention a number of times. For example, in the bass Anima's aria (no. 11b, m. 40), the melodic line descends at "Inferno" and ends on an E almost two octaves below middle C. In the same aria, the soul addresses the "cruel vortices of barbarous fire" and says, "Your ardor, like that of Hell, has become eternal." At "s'è fatto" ("become") there are almost sixteen measures of melisma (m. 60ff.). Finally, in Lucifero's last appearance (no. 31), he speaks of flying away *in a hurry* through the fire; appropriately, there is a long downward-moving melisma on the word "precipitoso."

Choruses

Some of the most interesting writing of the cantata occurs in the choral sections for the souls (nos. 5, 7, 9, 14, 16, 21, 25, 29, 32). Two of these sections include the soloists, Lucifero (no. 16) and Angelo (no. 32). At the beginning of the cantata, the souls plead for relief from the tortures of Lucifero; they cling to hope for the future. With the appearance of Angelo, however, the destiny of the souls changes; Heaven becomes a reality. Thus, by the end of the cantata, the souls are joyous. This change in their plight is reflected musically in the harmony and tonality, counterpoint, melodic lines, syncopation, and nonharmonic material. The tonality within the sections at the beginning tends to be unstable. Chords lack a sense of direction and key centers shift.[3] Not until the last two sections is the writing securely within the circle of fifths. This is the point at which the souls leave Purgatory for Paradise.

Tension is created in the choral sections through the use of counterpoint, a technique at which Stradella was particularly adept. In looking at one section in more detail, "Ah, che non dassi" (no. 14), we notice that the souls wonder why their suffering is not rewarded. This fugal section employs two subjects, and the initial entries for both subjects are presented as expositions of fugues. Another outstanding fugal section is "Pene rie" (no. 9), in which the souls beg that the horrible torture cease. After a five-measure introduction, the remaining fifteen measures present the subject numerous times. The counterpoint, coupled with excessive harmonic activity in a short period of time, creates a compact, intense movement.

The two sections in which dialogue occurs between the chorus and either Lucifero or Angelo are strategically placed within the work. The first section, "Mi consola" (no. 16) with Lucifero, rounds off the half that Lucifero dominates. In the brief recitative that follows (no. 17), Lucifero promises new rigors, but he is interrupted by the entrance of Angelo (no. 18). From that point on Angelo is in control. The second section with dialogue, "Alle gioie" (no. 32) with Angelo, occurs at the end of the half he dominates. In "Mi consola" the souls express hope for a time without suffering, but Lucifero promises pain. The key is C minor and the section ends on the dominant, almost as if more of the same torture follows. Within this section are several abrupt harmonic shifts, and at the end (m. 18ff.) is a brief reference, both textually and musically, to an earlier choral section, "Pene rie" (no. 9). "Alle gioie" presents an entirely different picture. Angelo is taking the souls to Paradise; they rejoice that they are leaving the torture. The choral sections, the solo, and the violins are well balanced, and tonally the section is securely in the home key of D major.

Instrumental Sections

The two-movement introductory sinfonia uses no material from the cantata. Since it originally circulated as two movements of an independent four-movement sinfonia, it is possible, though not certain, that the movements were borrowed for this cantata. It is interesting to note that in the oratorio *La Susanna*,[4] Stradella's other work whose introductory sinfonia circulated as an independent piece, there is no relationship between the music of the sinfonia and

---

3. It is interesting to note that the arias for the soprano Anima (no. 6) and the bass Anima (no. 11b), which are situated early in the work amid much choral writing, also reflect some of the instability so evident in the choral sections prior to Angelo's appearance.

4. I/MOe: Mus. F. 1137.

that of the oratorio. *Esule dalle sfere*'s sinfonia is typical of first and second (or last) movements of independent instrumental works.[5] The first movement has an introductory homophonic phrase repeated at the dominant. The following contrapuntal section presents a musical idea, then works it out in all parts. Both sequential treatment and doubling at the third, advanced techniques for Stradella, may be found. The second movement is a *siciliano* that employs cadences ending on weak beats. It has one theme, which is treated contrapuntally in all parts. Both movements are tonally secure in that they employ closely related keys, mainly the tonic, dominant, and subdominant.

The three ritornellos that occur within the cantata as separate units (nos. 10, 15, 30) contain ten, twenty, and fourteen measures respectively. Marked *ritornello* in the score, each is a self-contained unit that borrows material, sometimes almost exactly, from the choral section that precedes it. The cantata also contains other instrumental ritornellos, but they are integral parts of the sections in which they occur.

Thus, a detailed examination of the recitatives, arias, choruses, and instrumental sections of *Esule dalle sfere* reveals not only Stradella's sensitivity to the text but also his architectural genius.[6]

---

5. For a description of Stradella's style of writing in the instrumental works, see McCrickard, "Temporal and Tonal Aspects of Stradella's Instrumental Music."

6. For a more extensive treatment of this topic, see Eleanor F. McCrickard, "Stradella's *Esule dalle sfere*: A Structural Masterpiece," in *Atti del convegno internationale Alessandro Stradella: Siena 1982*, a volume of *Chigiana*, currently in press. For a description of Stradella's architectural genius in other works, see Dietz, "Musikalische Struktur und Architektur im Werke Stradellas"; Gianturco, "Caratteri stilistici delle opere teatrali di Stradella"; and Ziino, "Osservazioni sulla struttura de *L'Accademia d'Amore* di Stradella."

The Performance of
Esule dalle sfere

An authentic performance of *Esule dalle sfere* depends not only on the use of an edition that interprets the manuscript copies accurately, but also on a knowledgeable interpretation of the many aspects of Baroque music performance not indicated on the printed page. A basic knowledge of Baroque performance practices is assumed; this chapter will therefore concentrate on certain problems connected with the performance of this cantata rather than on generalities. Problems will not be solved; indeed, in many instances there is insufficient knowledge on which to base an authentic interpretation. Rather, certain problems in their complexity will be presented, and one editor's solution based on the material currently available will be given.

The two problems discussed in greatest detail are the selection of instruments for performing the cantata (especially the continuo instruments) and the realization of the continuo line. Other problems concern the selection of voices, ornamentation of vocal and instrumental lines, tempo, dynamics, and articulation.

Selection of Instruments

The only instrument named in the score is the violin, for which there are two parts. Whether or not there should be one or more players per part may be considered and should be determined to some extent by the balance in the group performing the cantata. One performer per part is quite satisfactory provided the chorus has no more than two or three voices per part. The choice of continuo instruments presents the greatest problem since there are no specific designations in the score. Clearly dispelled by now is the once-held belief that two instruments, cello or gamba and harpsichord or organ, should always be employed for the continuo. In his study on the basso continuo in seventeenth-century Italian music, Tharald Borgir makes the following points: At no time during the seventeenth century did there exist a general practice of employing chordal and bass-line instruments for the basso continuo. This fact is substantiated by his examination of both theoretical literature and music from the period. Scores rarely indicate which instruments were used. The fact that throughout the century separate parts may be found for bass-line instruments in opera scores and later in oratorio scores suggests that the basso continuo was played by both chordal and bass-line instruments, first in opera and later in oratorio.[1] In instrumental music the use of both bass-line and chordal instruments was confined to church sonatas, and then only when the part was contrapuntal in order to bring out melodic material.[2] For choral polyphony, the practice of using only one instrument for the continuo did not change throughout the seventeenth century and well into the eighteenth.[3] Around 1670 the addition of a bass-line instrument was suggested by a stylistic change originating in the opera aria and transferred to arias of other genres. The bass line, which had been slow moving and devoid of melodic interest prior to about 1670, became more important melodically in that thematic material and solo passages were played by the continuo.[4]

One can find examples of cantatas that include separate bass lines for the chordal and bass-line instruments. For example, in the Stradella cantata *Tante perle*, one aria, "Chi provo," has, in addition to the vocal and continuo lines, an obbligato line that is a more elaborate version of the continuo line.[5] Fran-

---

1. Borgir, "Performance of the Continuo," pp. 241–42.
2. Ibid., p. 54.
3. Ibid., p. 28.
4. Ibid., pp. 116–19.
5. Ibid., pp. 121–23; Jander, *Alessandro Stradella*, WECIS fasc. 4a, no. 138.

cesco Gasparini specifically states in the preface to *Cantate da camera a voce sola*, op. 1 (Rome, 1695), that some arias have two basses.[6] Likewise, the inclusion of a more elaborate version of a continuo line was not uncommon in instrumental works of the last quarter of the century. Two of Stradella's twenty-six instrumental ensemble works and Henry Purcell's two collections of sonatas (1683, 1697) contain two bass lines, as do works by Lelio Colista, Giovanni Maria Bononcini, Giovanni Battista Vitali, and Giuseppe Torelli. It therefore appears that the practice of using a bass-line as well as a chordal instrument was beginning to take hold in Italy during the last third of the century.

An examination of works in the Stradella sources similar to *Esule dalle sfere*, the sacred cantatas and oratorios, does not reveal much pertinent information regarding the selection of instruments. Some instruments are named for certain specific sections, but no clues are given as to how many instruments are used nor is an extra part included for a bass-line instrument.[7]

Although there is no clear evidence that *Esule dalle sfere* should have a bass-line instrument, it was written at a time when both chordal and bass-line instruments were beginning to be used together in cantatas and in instrumental music. Thus one must turn to internal evidence to see if the bass line warrants use of a bass-line instrument.

In several sections of *Esule dalle sfere*, the bass line is quite active, and in the sections scored for two violins, it is of equal importance to other parts. For example, in the introductory sinfonia, the bass line presents thematic material just as the violins do. In fact, in three places in the second movement, the bass line sounds alone as the lead voice in presenting thematic material. In the contrapuntal choruses all voice parts are of equal importance, and the continuo line doubles the bass line of the chorus but is less elaborate. In recitative sections, however, the bass lines, more harmonic in nature, provide a chordal foundation for the voice. This editor believes the internal evidence is strong enough to justify adding the bass-line instrument, especially in sections where violins are included and possibly in sections with more active bass lines. The particular acoustical situation for the specific performance may well influence a decision.

In addition to determining how many instruments should be employed for the continuo, one must also determine specifically the instruments to be used. The harpsichord and organ, the most popular keyboard instruments during Stradella's time, were not used exclusively for secular and sacred music respectively, as is sometimes assumed. Payment records indicate harpsichordists were employed both on a regular basis and for special events at some churches in Rome.[8] A set of playing parts for Stradella's sacred dialogue *Pugna certamen* includes a part for an *organo*,[9] whereas sections within scores for two other sacred works, the oratorio *San Giovanni Battista* and the cantata *Ah! troppo è ver*, specify a *cembalo*.[10] (Of course, this does not preclude the use of an organ too.) Regardless of the different types of instruments that the word *cembalo* could have indicated, it did not designate an organ. The editor is inclined to believe that the harpsichord is better suited for *Esule dalle sfere*.

---

6. Rose, "Clue from Gasparini," p. 29. This part of the preface is also cited in Borgir, "Performance of the Continuo," p. 123.

7. In addition to *Esule dalle sfere*, the sacred cantatas are *Da cuspide ferrate, Si apra al riso ogni labbro, Crudo mar di fiamme orribili*, and *Ah! troppo è ver*. The first three works do not name an instrument in their scores, but employ two violins and continuo. *Ah! troppo è ver*, an elaborate work for six solo voices and a four-part chorus, is accompanied by a concertino and concerto grosso. The instruments *leuto, cimbalo*, and *arpa doppia* are specifically named in a manuscript source to accompany certain sections (I/MOe: Mus. F. 1145). *Pugna certamen, militia est vita*, designated *dialogo* in the sources, is similar in some respects to the cantata, but it has a Latin text. Scored for four solo voices accompanied by concertino and concerto grosso, it has a set of playing parts designated *violino, viola*, and *organo* (I/MOe: Mus. F. 1126). Of Stradella's six extant oratorios—*Ester, liberatrice del popolo ebreo; Santa Edita, vergine e monaca, regina d'Inghilterra; San Giovanni Grisostomo; San Giovanni Battista; Santa Pelagia*; and *La Susanna*—the first three have only basso continuo. In the first two of these, the indications for *ritornello* suggest that other instruments were used. Two oratorios, *Santa Pelagia* and *La Susanna*, employ two violins and continuo, but only in the score for *La Susanna* are violins actually named. The most elaborate instrumentation is found in *San Giovanni Battista*, which calls for concertino and concerto grosso. One of the numerous copies of the oratorio (I/MOe: Mus. F. 1136) names a *cimbalo* and a *leuto* in certain places; another copy (I/Bc: BB362) designates *violino, viole*, and *violoncello*.

8. See, for example, lists included in Liess, "Materialien zur römischen Musikgeschichte des Seicento," and Wessely-Kropik, *Colista*.

9. I/MOe: Mus. F. 1126.

10. I/MOe: Mus. F. 1136 and I/MOe: Mus. F. 1145, respectively. See n. 7.

Should a bass-line instrument be included, one would have to decide on the specific instrument. Although the gamba was still preferred in many countries, Italy seems to have been the first country to develop preference for the cello.[11] In the mid-seventeenth century, bowed bass instruments were lacking in Rome, the archlute being the bass instrument used in ensembles around 1660.[12] One of the sources for Stradella's oratorio *San Giovanni Battista* (first performed in Rome in 1675) designates a violoncello for certain sections with a bass line florid in style. However, the date of this manuscript copy is not known; performance instructions may well have been added at a later date.[13] The cello is specifically mentioned in Gasparini's preface to his *Cantate da camera* (Rome, 1695).[14]

Facts surrounding the emergence of the violoncello in Italy are not altogether clear. As early as the 1560s and 1570s, the instrument many scholars would call the *violoncello* was produced by instrument makers in Italy. However, this term was not employed for another century, according to Stephen Bonta's intriguing article, "From Violone to Violoncello."[15] Although Bonta is primarily concerned with Bologna, where the violoncello was first encountered, he indicates that records in Rome provide evidence that the progression of events was the same there.[16] The *violone* was used in context of a *contrabasso*, then at some point the violoncello was played by the same performer.[17] The use of the term *violoncello* in Roman records, however, apparently dates from the last decade of the seventeenth century at the earliest, after *Esule*'s date (1680). Regardless of the characteristics or name of the instrument that played *Esule*,

the editor believes that the cello would be most satisfactory for a modern performance of this work, provided, of course, that it is not played too heavily.

Finally, regarding the selection of instruments, the modern performer must be cognizant of the violin, cello, and harpsichord that were used in Italy around 1680. Because Baroque violins and cellos and their bows were constructed differently from the instruments and bows used today, the sound was different. The harpsichord used in Italy in the seventeenth century had a single manual of about four octaves and two sets of strings, both at eight-foot pitch;[18] stops at the four-foot pitch appear irregularly. The technical differences between seventeenth-century and modern instruments and the modern performer's approach to Baroque music played on modern instruments are important problems, but they go beyond the scope of this chapter.[19]

Realization of the Continuo

One of the most difficult problems in dealing with performance practices concerns the realization of the continuo line. Research is still relatively young in this area, and in the work that has been done, there is a tendency to treat the Baroque as one broad period regardless of specific place, time, or genre. In order to determine what a realization of *Esule dalle sfere* should sound like, it is useful to study the theoretical and musical sources that are available to ascertain what hints are given for realizations for the cantata in Italy during the seventeenth century, especially around 1680. A comprehensive study is beyond the scope of this chapter, but the following comments may prove helpful.

SOURCES

In surveying the primary source material for Italy,[20] one immediately notices a number of treatises that

---

11. Donington (*Interpretation of Early Music*, pp. 362–63, 529) points out that Italy was probably the first country to develop a preference for the cello, but unfortunately he gives neither specific dates for the seventeenth century nor places within Italy.

12. Wessely-Kropik, *Colista*, p. 33.

13. The instructions appear to be by a different hand. For a discussion of the manuscript copy (I/Bc: BB362), see Daniels, "San Giovanni Battista," 1:27–28.

14. Rose, "Clue from Gasparini," p. 29.

15. Bonta, "From Violone to Violoncello," p. 64.

16. Records of musical activities in Rome that Bonta used include those in Leiss, "Materialien zur römischen Musikgeschichte des Seicento," pp. 144–66; and Marx, "Musik am Hofe Ottobonis unter Corelli," pp. 125–56, 169.

17. Bonta, "From Violone to Violoncello," p. 80. Bonta further discusses the complexities involving terminology, sizes, and tuning of instruments.

18. Hubbard, *Three Centuries of Harpsichord Making*, p. 28.

19. The construction of the violin has been treated in Boyden, *The History of Violin Playing*; that of the harpsichord, in Hubbard, *Three Centuries of Harpsichord Making*, pp. 1–42. The performance of early music on modern stringed instruments has been addressed by Donington in *String Playing in Baroque Music*.

20. This theoretical survey is limited primarily to writings of the theorists recorded in the monumental study by Arnold, *Thorough-Bass*.

date from the beginning of the seventeenth century.[21] Several years elapsed before the publication of the treatise closest in date to Stradella's compositions, Lorenzo Penna's *Li primi albori musicali* (3 bks., Bologna, 1672; reprinted in 1674, 1678 [bk. 2], 1679, 1684, 1696). Even though the dates of publication are within the period of Stradella's music, the applicability of the work may be questioned. Penna, who had close associations with the church and was an organist, was a conservative composer; on the contrary, Stradella was a progressive one. Because of this, Penna's suggestions for continuo realization may reflect an earlier style of composition than that of Stradella. Furthermore, one may wonder whether Penna was thinking in general terms with regard to realization of the continuo or specifically with only the organ in mind. It appears that in book 3, the book that treats figured bass, he evidently had the organ in mind. Even though the words *organo ò clavicembalo* appear on the title page for the three-volume set and therefore would include the contents of book 3, Penna uses the word *organo* alone on the title page for book 3.[22] The question, then, would be whether Penna's style of realization for organ would also suffice for harpsichord, which is the editor's preference for *Esule*.

Another source for studying the realization of the continuo line is Francesco Gasparini's *L'armonico pratico al cimbalo* (Venice, 1708). Even though it was published some twenty-eight years after the Stradella cantata, Gasparini had direct contacts with contemporaries of Stradella in the Roman school. A composer, performer, and teacher, Gasparini was said to have been a pupil of Bernardo Pasquini and Arcangelo Corelli in Rome. He worked specifically with cantatas of Pasquini, Giovanni Bononcini, and Alessandro Scarlatti.[23] In fact, his treatise was undoubtedly based on Pasquini's teachings.[24] Thus it may be seen that Gasparini worked at a time late enough to include comprehensive treatment of the mature Baroque style, yet early enough to avoid the intricate, extravagant procedures of the mid-eighteenth century.[25] Although the treatise reflects a somewhat more formulated style than that of Stradella, the assessment of Gloria Rose is convincing: "To those concerned with realizing the bass of 17th-century Italian music, *L'armonico pratico* may well be the most useful of all thorough-bass treatises."[26]

In addition to these main theoretical sources about basso continuo,[27] some music examples of varying types give hints as to how realizations were made. These, however, are mostly in manuscript form and not easily accessible. For example, manuscript copies of some of Stradella's own works occasionally give an extra part that imitates one of the other parts for a measure or two. Although Stradella does not follow this practice in *Esule dalle sfere*, his soprano solo cantatas, for example, contain many such instances.[28] A cantata by Alessandro Scarlatti, *Da sventura a sventura* (1690), has a written-out realization that is fairly simple, has three to five voices, and weaves fragments from the solo into the accompaniment.[29]

21. The earliest reported in Arnold is Lodovico Viadana's *Cento concerti* (1602), in which "twelve rules" discuss the performance of works, in particular the continuo (pp. 2–4, 9–19). In *Del suonare sopra il basso con tutti stromenti* (1607), Agostino Agazzari divides instruments for the continuo into two groups, those of foundation and those of accompaniment; he then sets certain general principles for each group (pp. 67–74). Michael Praetorius has a chapter on basso continuo in the third volume of his *Syntagma Musicum* (1619). Although the work is of German origin, it also reflects practices in Italy, because Praetorius quotes freely from both Viadana and Agazzari (pp. 93–100). Also appearing early in the century are Francesco Bianciardi's small treatise *Breve regola per imparar a sonare sopra il basso con ogni sorti d'instrumento* (1607) and Adriano Banchieri's *Dialogo musicale* (1611). Bianciardi deals mainly with rules for playing from an unfigured bass (pp. 75–80); Banchieri, who claims not to be an authority on the topic, a "composer rather than an organist," presents his discussion in the form of a dialogue (pp. 82–90). Finally, from the early part of the century, there is Galeazzo Sabbatini's *Regola facile e breve per sonare sopra il basso continuo nell'organo, manacordo, ò altro simile stromento* (1628). Although published in 1669 in Rome where Stradella worked until 1677, the treatise is of little practical value because the second part, which was intended for the more advanced player, was either never written or lost. Moreover, the examples in the existing part rarely represent anything likely to be encountered in actual practice, according to Arnold (p. 126). It is not clear how much influence these treatises from the first part of the century would have exerted on realizations around 1680.

22. Penna, *Li primi albori musicali*, pp. A1, 144.

23. Gasparini, *Practical Harmonist*, p. viii.
24. Arnold, *Thorough-Bass*, p. 250.
25. Gasparini, *Practical Harmonist*, p. viii.
26. Rose, "Clue from Gasparini," p. 29.
27. A small treatise called "Libro de primi elementi" (I/Bc: E66) bears the name Alessandro Stradella. It appears to be an elementary harmony book defining intervals, proportions, tones, and semitones. Its exercises are criticized in the margins. However, the 1694 date of the treatise makes the small, inarticulate book suspect since Stradella died in 1682.
28. Chaikin, "Solo Soprano Cantatas," p. 37c.
29. I/Nc: MS 34.5.2, fols. 2–6. The date on the first page looks as

In Gasparini's *Cantate da camera* (1695), three of the twelve cantatas contain arias with written-out accompaniments.[30] These are melodically embellished in the upper part, and in each aria one type of melodic figuration dominates.

It will be helpful for this study of the realization of the keyboard part (with the harpsichord in mind) to examine the comments or music examples that relate to the following three specific topics: the relationship of the realization to the vocal line, the style of the realization, and characteristics of harpsichord style. Among other topics, the treatises discuss the movement of chords; and Gasparini, in particular, discusses the realization of unfigured bass. These topics, however, are beyond the scope of this survey.

THE RELATIONSHIP OF THE REALIZATION TO THE VOCAL LINE

Most sources indicate that the realization should be subordinate to the vocal line and not interfere with it. However, when the voice is quiet, as in ritornellos and at the ends of phrases, the instrumental part should take command by imitating the portion just sung or by improvising. If instruments are used, Penna suggests that the realization avoid movement so that they can be heard. He also says that with a soprano or contralto, one must not play above the vocal part; with a tenor, one may go above and remain above the vocal line but should not play the notes he is singing in the same octave. Of course, the accompaniment for bass is above the voice, but by avoiding motion at the same time, it does not interfere with the vocal line.[31] In his chapter on "diminution, embellishment, and adornment," Gasparini warns against playing an interval or figure the singer might use. He specifically instructs continuo players never to play the vocal part note for note or other upper composed parts for the violin and other instruments.[32] For the three accompanied cantatas in Gasparini's *Cantate da camera*, the accompaniment lies well below the vocal line.

On the other hand, both theoretical comments and music examples indicate that these general principles did not always hold true. At one point Penna contradicts another statement when he notes that in accompanying a soprano or alto, the upper part of the accompaniment is to "coincide with the voice part" or at least "follow its general outline,"[33] evidently to give support to a singer who is unsure of notes. In the Scarlatti cantata *Da sventura a sventura*, the melodic line and the accompaniment intertwine as if the vocal and instrumental parts were conceived as one unit; sometimes the voice is uppermost and sometimes the accompaniment.

A specific problem concerning doubling of the vocal line in the accompaniment is the treatment of a suspended interval. Penna suggests that dissonances at cadences can be accompanied with consonances of the written note. He mentions that such effects are desirable, "more especially when the composition is for several voices . . . for five or more."[34] However, only occasionally in the Scarlatti cantata does one find doubling of the vocal line in the accompaniment.

The use of counterpoint between vocal and instrumental parts is definitely suggested by the Stradella and Scarlatti music examples cited above, but theoretical sources do not often mention it. In fact, Gasparini explicitly states that his study deals not with counterpoint but with a manner of accompaniment; he assumes that a student already has a knowledge of counterpoint.[35] Because of the lack of theoretical comments concerning counterpoint, one wonders if the use of counterpoint between vocal and instrumental parts was exceptional and if it was notated because it was more difficult than improvisation at sight. Or perhaps the composer simply wished to indicate places where imitation may occur. Penna has interesting comments about accompanying the entrances of subjects in a fugue, a situation that arises in the choral sections of *Esule dalle sfere*. In book 3 he states that the accompanist should play "first with one finger, then with two, and so on, the actual notes of the principal parts, as they enter one by one, till all have entered."[36] However, in book 2 he indicates that "one can (if one pleases) make a new Bass, and

---

if it might have been changed. Twenty measures are quoted in Donington, *Performer's Guide to Baroque Music*, pp. 222–23. Several other cantatas by Scarlatti also have passages that are realized. See Hanley, "Scarlatti's *Cantate da camera*," p. 19.

30. See excerpts in Rose, "Clue from Gasparini," p. 28.
31. Arnold, *Thorough-Bass*, p. 153.
32. Gasparini, *Practical Harmonist*, p. 89.
33. Arnold, *Thorough-Bass*, p. 148.
34. Ibid., pp. 146–47.
35. Gasparini, *Practical Harmonist*, p. 102.
36. Arnold, *Thorough-Bass*, p. 150.

therewith accompany the parts until the entry of the Bass."[37]

THE STYLE OF THE REALIZATION

Concerning the realization's style, sources indicate that the continuo player should understand the character of the piece and then accompany it accordingly.[38] Variety of style seems to be desirable. Examples indicate that in addition to the use of chords to accompany a melody, one may also employ counterpoint or embellish the melody, as will be pointed out in the section on ornamentation. In general, contrary motion between the hands is best. Likewise, it is desirable to avoid consecutive perfect octaves and fifths, especially in extreme parts, and to have the hands and fingers close together.

As far as the number of voices in the realization is concerned, variety is again the answer. There definitely seems to be an awareness of balance between vocal and instrumental parts. Penna states that there should be at least four sounding parts, unless the bass goes high, when three will suffice. Later he says that in accompanying a single voice, the number of parts should not exceed three or, in exceptional cases, four parts. This rule does not apply to recitative style.[39] Whereas the Scarlatti cantata has from three to five voices, the Gasparini arias from the cantatas at times have only two.

That a full-voiced texture was used upon occasion in the seventeenth century cannot be denied. Quite early in the history of thorough-bass, composers used a fuller accompaniment than the normal three or four parts when the situation demanded it. Michael Praetorius, who relied heavily on the Italian tradition, even mentions this type of accompaniment as early as 1619 in his *Syntagma musicum*.[40] Penna says that the harmony should be full when there are eight voices or when there are three or four choirs; duplicate intervals and accidentally sharpened notes should be doubled.[41] In discussing chords with a minor seventh, Gasparini says that the fuller one makes these chords, the more harmony they will produce. He indicates that notes should be doubled in both the left and right hands. He goes on to say that with recitative, the more certain dissonances can be played full and doubled, the better the effect.[42]

Music examples showing a full-voiced texture also exist, but they date from some time after the Stradella cantata. In an anonymous manuscript (ca. 1700) in the Corsiniana Library in Rome, an arietta of seventy-six measures is realized in a full-voiced style that doubles numerous dissonances.[43] Around 1725 a realization of Corelli's op. 5 by Antonio Tonelli employs a full-voiced texture that includes all the notes the hands can encompass.[44] In his treatise of 1728, Johann Heinichen fully describes this essentially Italian style of accompanying that he first discovered in Venice, where he studied.[45] More extensive use of this full-voiced texture undoubtedly was a result of the growth of the orchestra employed in the large theatrical productions at the end of the century. Whether that texture should be used in *Esule dalle sfere* may well depend on balance in the particular performance. The Italian harpsichord of the time had only two eight-foot stops (with possibly an additional four-foot stop); if one registers for a modern performance accordingly, the use of additional notes in the accompaniment probably will be necessary, especially in the last chorus.

CHARACTERISTICS OF HARPSICHORD STYLE

This topic is of particular importance to anyone playing a realization today. An essential characteristic of harpsichord style is arpeggiation of chords. Penna advises players to arpeggiate the chords (presumably on the harpischord) in order not to leave a void in the instrument.[46] On the other hand, Gasparini warns against too much arpeggiation: "In order to perform the accompaniments of recitatives with some degree of good taste, the consonances must be deployed almost like an arpeggio, though not continuously so. Once the harmony of a note has been heard, one must hold the keys fast and permit the singer to take

---

37. Ibid.
38. Ibid., p. 151.
39. Ibid., pp. 136, 150, 153.
40. Buelow, *Thorough-Bass Accompaniment*, pp. 69–70.
41. Arnold, *Thorough-Bass*, p. 153.
42. Gasparini, *Practical Harmonist*, p. 79.
43. Landshoff, "Über das vielstimmige Accompagnement," pp. 189–93. This manuscript (I/Rli: Musica R1) is entitled "Regole per accompagnare sopra la parte."
44. I/MOe: Mus. F. 1174.
45. Buelow, "Full-voiced Style," p. 169.
46. Arnold, *Thorough-Bass*, p. 154.

the lead, singing at his discretion and in accord with the expression of the words. Do not annoy or disturb him with a continuous arpeggio, or with ascending or descending scale passages."[47]

The acciaccatura was also a characteristic of harpsichord style, especially in Italy. Dissonant notes added to arpeggios provided variety and "spice" in the accompaniments. Another characteristic of the style was the cadential trill, to be discussed in the section on ornamentation. Both variety and a personal touch can be added to an accompaniment through the numerous idiomatic characteristics of the harpsichord, details of which are best left to manuals that deal with the topic.[48]

In investigating the style of realization in the Italian cantata around 1680, one cannot help noticing the variety of possible realizations. Indeed, for the most satisfactory realizations, spontaneity in improvisation is a most important factor. It is no wonder that, after explaining how to make a realization, the seicento authors of treatises urged students to listen to the masters.[49]

Selection of Voices

Two soloists (soprano and bass) and a chamber chorus (the soprano and bass of which have solo parts) are employed in *Esule dalle sfere*. The score demands that Lucifero be a virtuoso bass whose voice has a range from G to e^1. Like many Lucifers of the seventeenth century, he has a quite demanding part that requires a voice both full and agile. It seems logical that originally castrati sang the parts of Angelo and the soprano Anima. The manuscript copies have soprano clefs for both parts. The practice of employing castrati to sing the high parts was prevalent not only at the Vatican chapel but throughout Italy because women were forbidden to sing in the Roman Catholic church. Today Angelo should be performed by a soprano with a light, agile voice whose range is c^1 to a^2 and Anima, by a soprano with a somewhat darker, heavier voice whose range is c^1 to g^2.

The bass Anima part calls for a voice with a wide range, from D to e^1. Because of its style and range, Stradella undoubtedly must have had a specific singer in mind for this part, which is found only in a secondary source, Mus. F. 1148 in the Biblioteca Estense at Modena. This bass part is similar to Lucifero's in that it is dramatic. In keeping with other choruses of the period, the Chorus of Souls should be small; two or three singers per part should be sufficient.

Vocal and Instrumental Ornamentation

Ornamentation as a part of the Baroque style is now taken for granted. However, the extent of ornamentation at a given time, in a given place, for works of a specific genre, is still debated. The eminent Baroque scholar, Nino Pirrotta, gives his views in this statement: "I am strongly opposed to any addition of vocal embellishments to the written scores of most seventeenth-century composers, except for some trills (possibly of the repeated-note type) and, later, for some appoggiaturas. The fact is that most composers wrote out ornaments wherever the situation required them."[50] Yet as one glances through scores and sees ornamentation written into the works, one cannot help believing that performers probably added ornamentation in some places, whether the composer liked it or not.

In Stradella's works one may find a limited amount of ornamentation written into the manuscript. An illustration may be found in an autograph of the serenata *Hor ch'alla dea notturna*, where ornamentation is added at the cadence in the manner shown in Example 1.[51] Examples of ornamentation for instrumental music also indicate added cadential activity in this way, as shown in Example 2.[52] Additional perusal of Stradella scores no doubt would reveal other examples.

---

47. Gasparini, *Practical Harmonist*, p. 79.

48. See Gasparini's discussion of the acciaccatura in chap. 9 of *Practical Harmonist* and Williams's discussions in *Figured Bass Accompaniment*, pp. 40–44, and in "The Harpsichord Acciaccatura."

49. Arnold, *Thorough-Bass*, p. 154; and Gasparini, *Practical Harmonist*, p. 88.

50. Pirrotta, "Early Opera and Aria," p. 65. Genre is a consideration at this point.

51. In addition to this autograph, other manuscripts of the serenata are GB/Lbm: RCM 604 and R.M.23.f.10[17] and GB/Cfm: 22 H 16.

52. There is no other copy of Mus. G. 210, no. 5, and the other copy of Mus. F. 1129, no. 11, does not have the cadential ornamentation. These works are published as nos. 8 and 17 respectively in McCrickard, *Alessandro Stradella*, pp. 54–59 and 140–50.

Example 1: Cadential Ornamentation in an Autographed Serenata

a. I/Vnm: Cod. It. IV-560, fol. 90

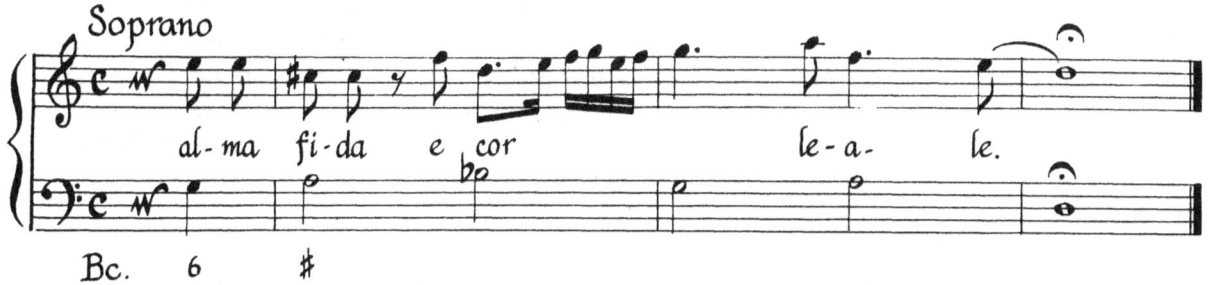

b. I/Vnm: Cod. It. IV-560, fol. 102

Example 2: Cadential Ornamentation in Two Instrumental Works

a. I/MOe: Mus. G. 210, no. 5, mvt. 1

b. I/MOe: Mus. F. 1129, no. 11, mvt. 2

Two types of ornaments were obligatory, the trill and the appoggiatura. Penna attached much importance to the trill. In fact, he evidently regarded the "shake" (trill) as the "proper adjunct of every form of cadence."[53] His examples indicate that the trill should begin on the note above the main note and close with the main note; at the close of the trill, the note below the main note is touched. There were many forms of the appoggiatura, involving variations in the length of duration, resolution up or down, and movement by step or leap.[54]

One might consider adding ornaments at other places in the cantata although theoretical information and music examples dating from around 1680 are lacking at present. Evidently the repetition of the A section in the ABA aria should be ornamented. In a French source, *Remarques curieuses sur l'art de bien chanter* (Paris, 1668), Bénigne de Bacilly suggests that repeated material should be ornamented: "Everyone agrees that the less one can make passages in the first verse, the better." The idea is that the ornamentation prevents the melody from being heard in its pure form.[55] In his *Opinioni de' cantori antichi, e moderni* (Bologna, 1723), Franceso Tosi says that "in repeating the *Air* [i.e., in the 'da capo'], he that does not vary it for the better, is no great Master."[56] The possibility of inserting a cadenza at the ends of the arias in *Esule dalle sfere* may also be taken into consideration.[57] There are examples of written-out cadenzas in the early Baroque works of Caccini and Monteverdi.[58] At the beginning of the eighteenth century, cadenzas must have been quite elaborate, since Tosi speaks of three in one aria, each of progressive difficulty.[59] Cadential activity in works by Stradella is evident in Examples 1 and 2.

One final type of Baroque ornamentation should be mentioned. Gasparini devotes one chapter (no. 10) to the "diminution, embellishment, and adornment of the accompaniment" and another (no. 11) to the "diminution or adornment of the bass." In addition to numerous musical examples given in his treatise, the three accompanied arias from the cantatas in his *Cantate da camera* show how the lines were melodically embellished.

Tempo, Dynamics, and Articulation

Finally, indications in the score for tempo, dynamics, and articulation are rare or nonexistent. Tempo markings are given only in the bass Anima recitative in the secondary source (no. 11a). Although circumstances of the specific performance determine to some extent the tempo, care must be taken that the performance of the cantata is not too slow. The recitatives, of course, should be taken somewhat freely with the text in mind. No dynamic markings are included in the cantata sources, and marks for articulation within the scores are rare. A hallmark of the style is the slurred cadence in which one voice enters a half beat before the other parts. (For example, notice the final cadence of *Esule dalle sfere*.) With the exception of this special slurred cadence, no articulation markings extend across the beat. The few markings in Stradella's instrumental works all begin on the beat. Indeed, the articulation must assure that the cantata sound vitally alive, a characteristic of all of Stradella's music regardless of genre.

Clearly, performance instructions in the score are rare with respect to the selection of instruments (especially continuo instruments), the realization of the continuo line, the selection of voices, the ornamentation of vocal and instrumental lines, and the tempo, dynamics, and articulation. An authentic performance of *Esule dalle sfere* ultimately depends on a knowledgeable interpretation of the many aspects of Baroque music not indicated on the printed page.

53. Arnold, *Thorough-Bass*, p. 134.
54. For a thorough explanation, see Donington, *Interpretation of Early Music*, pp. 236–59, 197–216; and *Performer's Guide to Baroque Music*, pp. 178–90, 195–203.
55. Donington, *Interpretation of Early Music*, p. 174.
56. This portion, from an English translation of Tosi's work entitled *Observations on the Florid Song*, p. 94, is quoted in Donington, ibid. Even though the book was published in 1723, over forty years after Stradella's death, Tosi, who was born only eight years after Stradella, was a contemporary and may well have reflected the same style as Stradella in his book.
57. For example, places within the arias where cadenzas may be inserted effectively include no. 4, m. 75; and no. 22, m. 86.
58. Donington, *Interpretation of Early Music*, p. 185.
59. See Tosi, *Opinioni* [*Observations on the Florid Song*], pp. 128–29.

The Present Edition

Sources

The two sources of *Esule dalle sfere* are both manuscript copies, but neither is the composer's autograph. The cantata has never before been published. Giordano 12, found in the Biblioteca Nazionale Universitaria in Turin, is the primary source; and Mus. F. 1148, found in the Biblioteca Estense in Modena, is the secondary source.[1]

The primary source also contains two other sacred cantatas. The title page, which identifies the subject, number of voice parts, and instrumentation of each cantata, reads thus: "Cantata per il S. Natale à 5 con V.[iolino] V.[iolino] / L'Anime del Purgatorio à Solo con V. V. / L'Anime del Purgatorio à 5 con V. V." In the index at the back of the volume, the following information is found: "Cantate / Del Sig[nor] Alessandro Stradella. / Ah Troppo è ver. Per il SS. Natale – [fol.] i. a5 con Strom[en]ti: / Crudo Mar. Per l'Anime del Purgat[ori]o: – [fol.] 65. B[asso]: Solo con Strom[en]ti: / Esule dalle Sfere. Per l'Anime del Purg[ato]rio – [fol.] 95. a5 con Strom[en]ti." These three cantatas are better known by their first lines as given in the index. Giordano 12 is an oblong volume (23.5 × 16.25 cm.) bound in brown leather with gold tooling. The scribe and the watermark on the paper have been identified as Roman.[2] At the top of the first page of *Esule dalle sfere*, the following inscription is found: "Cantata à.5. con Strom[en]ti / Per l'Anime del Purgatorio / Del Sig[no]r Aless[andr]o Stradella."

The secondary source for the cantata, Mus. F. 1148, contains only *Esule dalle sfere*. The title page for the volume reads as follows: "Cantata a 5. / Per l'anime del Purgatorio / Parole del Figari / Musica / d'Alessandro Stradella." At the top of the first page is the following inscription: "Cantata à 5 Per l'Anime del Purgatorio / Con gli Violini. / Del Sig:[no]r Al[e]s[sandr]o Stradella." The date 1680 is in the upper left corner. The outside cover of the oblong volume (20.3 × 27.3 cm.) is a multicolored marbled paper; the volume contains some seventy folios of music.

The sinfonia of this cantata also circulated as two movements of a four-movement instrumental work.[3] It is not known whether the two movements of the independent instrumental work were borrowed for the cantata or whether the two-movement introductory sinfonia was expanded to become an independent work. The instrumental work may be found in the following sources:[4]

I/Tn, Foà 11, fols. 53–60v
I/MOe, Mus. F. 1129, no. 8
I/Bc, Marino Silvani, *Scielta delle suonate* (Bologna: Giacomo Monte, 1680), no. 6: V. I, pp. 22–25; V. II, pp. 21–24; Bc., pp. 17–20
GB/Lbm, Add. 31436, fols. 153v–154, 172v–173, 192v–193

The history of the sources for the cantata becomes more vague the nearer to Stradella's time it is traced. The primary source in Turin, Giordano 12, is part of a large collection of sixteenth-, seventeenth-, and eighteenth-century music donated to the Biblioteca Nazionale Universitaria by the prominent Turin businessman, Filippo Giordano, in memory of his young son who died in early childhood.[5] The Stradella volume that contains *Esule dalle sfere* was acquired in 1930 from a descendant of the Durazzo family of Genoa, a family that had been in Genoa since the fourteenth century. The Stradella holdings of the Durazzo family totaled almost forty volumes; the

---

1. In determining primary and secondary sources, the editor has accepted the conclusions of a study of Stradella sources made by Jander, *Alessandro Stradella*, WECIS fasc. 4a, pp. 38–44.
2. Ibid., no. 160.
3. This work is no. 14, *Sinfonia* (D major), in McCrickard, *Alessandro Stradella*, pp. 115–21. The four-movement introductory sinfonia of Stradella's oratorio *La Susanna* (I/MOe: Mus. F. 1137) also circulated as an independent work.
4. See a comparison of all sources in McCrickard, *Alessandro Stradella*, pp. 277–78.
5. Gentili, "La raccolta di antiche musiche 'Renzo Giordano,'" pp. 117–25.

volume containing *Esule dalle sfere* was one of the five acquired in the Giordano collection. The history of the volume before the Durazzo family acquired it is not known. However, since Stradella had lived in Genoa for the four years before he was murdered in 1682, he may have been connected with that family either directly or through a mutual friend, possibly Anton Brignole-Sale, Stradella's principal patron.[6]

The secondary source in Modena, Mus. F. 1148, is from the largest existing Stradella collection, one that contains about forty manuscript copies. These volumes were produced by scribes, presumably for sale to the library of Francesco II d'Este. A letter dated 19 August 1682 in the Archivio di Stato in Modena, written by a secretary or librarian to Stradella's priest brother, indicates that the priest had gathered together his brother's manuscripts and was attempting to sell them to Francesco II in order to support Stradella's unidentified child.[7] Although the letter indicates the price was too high, an agreement was apparently reached because the large Stradella collection now exists in Modena. An early handwritten list (1682?) of Stradella's manuscripts in the Biblioteca Estense, possibly made shortly after Stradella's death, may concern the sale of the manuscript copies to the Este library.[8] It is interesting to note that in a nineteenth-century catalog of Stradella's works in that library, the librarian-cataloger labeled *Esule dalle sfere* a "composizione notevole." Such remarks are infrequent in this catalog.[9]

Editorial Procedures

This modern performing edition is based on the primary source of the cantata, Giordano 12. The secondary source, Mus. F. 1148, as well as additional sources for the introductory sinfonia, was examined and compared with the primary source. Any problems or differences between sources having direct bearing on the interpretation of the cantata have been presented in the following section, "Textual Comments and Variants."

In comparing the sources of the cantata, one finds that the secondary source is basically the same as the primary source except for the inclusion of a striking virtuoso recitative and aria for bass; these are designated in the manuscript copy for a soul from the chorus (*un'Anima del Coro–Basso*) and are included in this edition as 11a and 11b. In the secondary source, the arias for Angelo (nos. 22 and 26), Lucifero (nos. 3 and 4), and a soprano of the chorus (no. 8) are all labeled *aria*, and instructions as to when instruments perform are more explicit. No editorial comments are made about minor differences concerning text, slurs, ties, figures, accidentals, and fermatas unless one is of particular significance. Differences in the text underlay usually concern the repetitions that are written out and those that are indicated by a repeat sign. The use of slurs in Mus. F. 1148 and Giordano 12 varies considerably; in particular, the typical figure at the end of a phrase (the weak beat carrying the syllable that is slurred into a strong beat) usually has no slur in Mus. F. 1148.

The musical items are numbered to serve as points of reference and to facilitate discussion of the cantata. The numbering is usually determined by the location of double bars in the manuscript copy and is almost always coincidental with a change in performer. Because of the style of this work, in which recitatives merge into ariosolike passages and even into arialike passages, no divisions are named except the sinfonia and ritornellos, so designated in both sources. Within each division of the music, every fifth measure is numbered, beginning with the first full measure.

The text that is used within the edition has been lightly edited with respect to accents and capitalization to conform more closely to modern Italian usage. Archaic words have been retained, but spelling has been modernized. Elisions have been marked in the performance score. As is usual for the period, the text underlay is not precise, but it does not present problems. Repetition of text may be indicated by a sign. No comments are made about the placement of these signs because no problems are involved. Almost all punctuation has been added because the sources have very little.

All editorial additions to the score (accidentals and figures, for example) have been placed in brackets or, in the case of ties and slurs, have been dashed. Obvious errors have been corrected without comment.

Modern clefs have been employed throughout the edition. In the sources the two soprano parts, Angelo

---

6. Jander, *Alessandro Stradella*, WECIS fasc. 4a, p. 25.
7. Hess, *Die Opern Stradella's*, p. 2. Recent research does not reveal that Stradella had a child.
8. Jander, *Alessandro Stradella*, WECIS fasc. 4a, p. 15.
9. Catelani, *Delle opere di Stradella*, p. 22.

and the soprano Anima (originally castrati parts?), utilize soprano clef; Lucifero and the bass Anima, bass clef; the four-part chorus, soprano, alto, tenor, and bass clefs; the two violins, treble clef; and the continuo, with the exception of one section, bass clef. Because of the use of modern clefs and notation and because there are no problems concerning clefs, the editor has neither presented an incipit for each section nor noted clef changes within a section.

The manuscript copies use modern time signatures that agree with the notation for the most part. However, sections with the signatures 3/8, 3/4, and 3/2 usually have some measures that belong to the signatures 6/8, 6/4, and 6/2 respectively. Bar-lines have been added without comment to make the signature and measures agree. Dots across bar-lines and the placement of beams and stems of notes have been modernized.

In the cantata sources the intention of the composer with respect to accidentals is almost always clear. Normally the accidental affects only the note against which it is placed; if the note is repeated later in the measure, so is the accidental. No comment is made with respect to accidentals unless a problem of interpretation exists. In the manuscript copies a flat lowers a note and a sharp raises it. Therefore, in the edition a natural replaces the sharp or flat without comment.

The few figures that appear in the manuscript copies above, below, or on the continuo line have been placed below the continuo line in this edition with the higher number on top and any accidental preceding the number. Although no attempt has been made to provide all figures needed to show all the movement of vocal and instrumental lines, enough figures have been added in brackets so that a performer may quickly realize the basso continuo without having to rely heavily on the vocal and instrumental lines. A blank staff has been provided for the performer's sketch of a realization if one should be desired.

Textual Comments and Variants

The following order has been used with respect to textual comments and variants: the number of the section; the measure number within that section; an abbreviation of the voice or instrument (Angelo—Ang., Lucifero—Luc., Chorus—SATB, Violino I or II—V. I or II, Basso continuo—Bc.); the number of the note within the measure about which there is a comment; and the comment. The primary source is indicated by T (I/Tn: Giordano 12); the secondary source, by M (I/MOe: Mus. F. 1148). Other sources for the introductory sinfonia, taken from the independent instrumental sources, have been written out.

[1] Mvt. 1: No tempo markings are given in any source; however, several instrumental sinfonias that follow the same form indicate either *adagio* for the introductory homophonic section or *allegro* for the contrapuntal section that follows.

13, V. I, note 6: M has f#^{2}.

15, Bc., note 5: A sharp is in Silvani and Add. 31436.

16, V. I, note 2: M has no accidental; T has no accidental for note 5.

19, V. II, note 8: No independent instrumental source has a sharp.

20, V. I, note 5: M has no sharp.

23, V. II, note 2: Mus. F. 1129 has no sharp.

27: The single bar following the measure in T indicates that the sinfonia is considered one unit.

Mvt. 2: In Silvani and Add. 31436 this movement is third and is in 3/2.

5–6, V. II: Notes in Silvani and Add. 31436 are d^2 e^2 d^2 a^1 b^1 a^1; Bc.: d d c# d.

6–7, Bc.: Notes in Foà 11 and Mus. F. 1129 are f# c# d B A; 3 eighth notes are in m. 6.

19, Bc., note 3: Silvani and Add. 31436 have no sharp.

24–27, Bc.: Notes of mm. 24–25 in Silvani and Add. 31436 repeat the rhythmic pattern found in mm. 26–27; notes for the four measures are e e a f b c^1 b g.

[2] 11, Bc., note 2: M omits the sharp in the figures.

18, Luc., note 2: M has c#.

18, Luc., last note: T has c#^{1}; M is not clear.

[4] 1, Bc., note 7: This is the only place in both sources where a sharp precedes g.

[6] 10–11, Bc., notes 2–1: M has a tie.

[8]	65, Bc., note 2: T and M both have f.
	84, V. I and Bc., last notes: The use of g# and g simultaneously occurs occasionally in Stradella's compositions.
	89, V. I: M has a².
	111, Bc.: Note values are reversed in both T and M. Cf. m. 16.
[9]	1, B.: The two notes are without text in either manuscript copy of the cantata. There appears to be a whole rest above the two notes.
	5, S., notes 1–2: In M the slur is between notes 1 and 2 rather than notes 2 and 3.
	13–14, A.: A second "non più" is inserted in M and takes up two syllables belonging to "rigori."
	15, A., note 1 (following tied d¹): The edition follows M; T has d¹.
	17, A., note 1: The edition follows M; T has a¹.
[11b]	The double bar with dots on both sides that follows m. 14 in the source has been interpreted as a repeat sign for the first section only. Note how subsequent phrases are repeated.
	7, B., notes 3–4: The slur appears to be over notes 3–4 rather than 2–3. Cf. m. 9, a clear example.
[12]	1–2, Bc.: In M the notes are tied.
[14]	Throughout the chorus there is inconsistency in both sources as to use of "ah" and "ahi."
	28, A., note 1: T and M have e¹.
	36, S., notes 1–2: M has a slur.
	57, T., notes 1–2: The slur is from M.
	58: M indicates *Ritornello subito segue*.
[15]	8, 19: M has a slur over all the notes in V. I in mm. 8 and 19 and over the first two notes of V. II in m. 8.
[16]	Lucifero's part is above the continuo in both sources.
	5, S., note 4: M has no accidental.
	16–17, Luc.: The text in both manuscripts has "dei" rather than "devi." The melodic line has been adjusted to accommodate the extra syllable.
	19, beat 1: All vocal parts are from M; T allowed for only one syllable (two in V. I) because the text reads "crudel."
[17]	3: M has whole notes.
[21]	22, A.: The rhythm is a dotted whole note in M.
[22]	4, V. I, note 6: M has b². Cf. m. 60 in both sources.
	15, Ang., notes 1–2: The slur is from M (it also occurs in m. 29, Ang., notes 2–4; m. 31, V. II, notes 1–2; m. 50, Ang., notes 5–6, 7–9).
	35, Ang., notes 7–9: The length of the slur in this and other similar places has been extended to include the third note. The sources are not always clear as to the placement of slurs.
[25]	Bc. is omitted in M.
[28]	2–3, Bc., notes 2–1: The tie is from M.
[29]	28, S., note 3: T has g¹.
[31]	6, Luc., note 9: Both T and M have a sharp; perhaps it is intended for the preceding note.
	7, Bc., note 1: The meaning of the figures ♭7 in T is not clear. M has ♭⅗.
[32]	38–39, A.: The text underlay problem in T is solved in M. Because no slur occurs in m. 38, "già" is placed under note 3 and "sva-" takes the next measure.
	57, Bc., note 1: M has a variant version, c#, a dotted half note.

Text of *Esule dalle sfere*

The Text in Modernized Form

Cantata a 5 con strumenti

Per l'anime del Purgatorio

Del Signor Alessandro Stradella

An English Translation

Cantata a 5[1] with Instruments

For the Souls of Purgatory

By Alessandro Stradella

Text attributed to Pompeo Figari[2]

Transcribed and translated by Aldo Scaglione[3]

Voices:
Angelo (Angel)—Soprano
Lucifero (Lucifer)—Bass
Anime (Souls)—Chorus (Soprano, Alto, Tenor, Bass)
Anima (Soul)—Solo Parts for Soprano and Bass from Chorus

[1] Sinfonia

[2] Lucifero

Esule dalle sfere[4]
poi ch'indarno bramai l'Etereo
  Trono,
il mio vasto pensiere
a restringer tra l'ombre astretto io
  sono;
ma tanti oltraggi
e tanti lasciar invendicati
io già non voglio.
Questi spirti purganti destinati
a calcar quei seggi istessi
onde i seguaci miei furon depressi,
bersaglio de' miei sdegni,
delle vendette mie portino i segni!

Exiled from the spheres since I in vain desired the Celestial Throne, I am condemned to constrain my vast thoughts here among the shadows. But so many outrages I do not want to leave unavenged; let these spirits being purged, destined to occupy those same seats from which my followers were cast out, the target of my scorn, let them carry the marks of my revenge.

[3] Mie schiere severe, vendetta! Sù, sù!

Up, up, my fearful hordes, to revenge!

---

1. The meaning of *a 5* is not clear. It appears in both sources, yet the vocal performing forces in the secondary source number only five, provided one considers all soloists separately and the chorus collectively: Lucifero, Angelo, Anime (SATB chorus), Anima [S], and Anima [B].

2. Designation of Figari as librettist comes from the secondary source.

3. Dr. Aldo Scaglione is W. R. Kenan, Jr., Professor of Romance Languages and Comparative Literature at the University of North Carolina at Chapel Hill.

4. Giordano 12, the primary source, has "delle" rather than "dalle." The editor employs "dalle" from the secondary source because the meaning of the title is better reflected by "dalle." A copyist may well have substituted "delle." The title of the work is well circulated as *Esule dalle sfere*.

[4]	Questi a noi fatti rivali della gloria in farsi sposi, pria ch'al Cielo impennin l'ali proveranno, scorgeranno quanto possano gelosi i Luciferi qua giù.	These who have been made our rivals in wedding themselves to glory, they will experience, they will see the power of the jealous Lucifers down here, before they wing their way to Heaven.
	Mie schiere severe, vendetta! Sù, sù!	Up, up, my fearful hordes, to revenge!
[5] Anime	Da mostri sì crudeli, soccorso, per pietà! Soccorso, o Cieli!	Oh heavens, do help (us) for pity's sake from such cruel monsters!
[6] Anima [S]	Misera, sventurata anima tormentata, in duolo eterno aver dunque degg'io alle gioie del Ciel strada un Inferno? Deh, mio Signor, mio Dio, non tolerar ch'inferociti, irati, questi dal Ciel scacciati empi tiranni dispongano a sua voglia i nostri affanni.	Oh wretched, unfortunate, tormented soul, must I then have, in eternal grief, a hell as my path to the joys of heaven? Pray, oh my Lord, my God, do not allow these impious tyrants, who were cast out from heaven and are now ferocious and wrathful, to dispose our sufferings at their will.
[7] Anime	Da mostri sì crudeli, soccorso, per pietà! Soccorso, o Cieli!	Oh heavens, do help (us) for pity's sake from such cruel monsters!
[8] Anima [S]	Troppo avari siete, o Cieli, dei contenti.	You are too miserly, oh heavens, with your blessings.
	Troppo amari li rendete se sì cari li vendete solo a prezzo di tormenti.	You make them too bitter, if you sell them so dearly only at the price of torments.
	Troppo avari siete, o Cieli, dei contenti.	You are too miserly, oh heavens, with your blessings.
[9] Anime	Pene rie, crudi ardori, cessate! Per pietà, non più rigori!	Horrible pains, cruel burning, cease! For pity's sake, no more rigors!
[10] Ritornello		
[11] Lucifero	Non ancor a bastanza, o forsennati, provaste i miei furori;	Not yet enough, oh wretched ones, have you felt my fury; I aspire to torment you with such great pain

	con sì gran pene a tormentarvi aspiro che vuò che nell'udirle ancor dei sdegni miei tremi l'Empiro.	that, upon hearing of them, I want the Empyrean still to tremble at my scorn.
[11a] Anima [B]	No, no, non più rigori o pene rie, ci costan troppo care le gioie dell'Empiro, se sì crudi tormenti farsi sentiero all'alta mole io miro.	No, no, no more rigors, oh terrible pains. The joys of the Empyrean cost us too dear if I gaze upon such cruel torments becoming the pathway to the high place.
	Non più rigori, oh Dio. Ma se pure infierite, sempre v'incrudelite, nè impietosirvi al mio pregar volete, io vel concedo, o rie.	No more rigors, oh God. But if you go on with your cruelty nor do you turn to pity on my prayer, I resign myself to you, oh wicked ones.
	Sù, sù, crescete, accendete, abbruciate, saziatevi al fin. Ma poi cessate.	Up, up, grow, flare up, burn, satisfy yourselves at last. But then, cease.
[11b]	Crude voragini di foco barbaro, cessate un dì, che fiere imagini d'un altro Tartaro il nume alato[5] in voi ci apri, mentre al par dell'Inferno scorgo ch'il vostro ardor s'è fatto eterno.	Cruel vortices of barbarous fire, cease one day. Let the winged god open for us fiery images of another Hell while I perceive that your ardor, like that of Hell, has become eternal.
[12] Anima [S]	Carnefici spietati, saziatevi pur, ch'al fin prefisso è che termini un dì per noi l'abisso; e la speme del porto ancor fra le tempeste è un gran conforto.	Pitiless tormentors, satiate yourselves now because it is destined in the end that the abyss shall one day terminate for us, and the hope of reaching port is a great comfort even in the tempest.
[13] Lucifero	Anzi rendervi io spero con la speranza ogni dolor più fiero!	On the contrary, I trust that through your own hope I will render each pain sharper.

5. In repetition of the text, "irato" is used.

[14]	Anime	Ahi, che non dassi, oh Dio, di sperato gioir martir più rio!	Oh God, there is no harsher suffering than long-delayed rejoicing!
[15]	Ritornello		
[16]	Anime	Mi consola amica spene.	Friend Hope comforts me.
	Lucifero	Ma non mancano le pene!	But pain is not lacking!
	Anime	Dunque, ahi lasse! e che sarà? Finiran l'alte sciagure?	Then, oh unfortunate ones, what will happen? Will the great sufferings end?
	Lucifero	Ma fra tanto son più dure!	But in the meantime they are even harsher!
	Anime	Sommo nume, oh Dio, pietà! Un dì godrò.	Highest Lord, oh God, pity! One day I shall be blessed.
	Lucifero	Ma devi purgar gl'errori!	But you must purge your sins!
	Anime	Non più, mostri crudeli, non più rigori!	No more, oh cruel monsters, no more rigors!
[17]	Lucifero	Nuove forme di pene machina un giusto sdegno.	A just indignation creates new forms of pain.
[18]	Angelo	Frena, o dell'alto Iddio ribelle indegno, frena, frena l'audace lingua e l'ardor de' purganti oggi s'estingua.	Stop, oh unworthy rebel to the Highest God, stop, stop the audacious tongue, and may the burning of the purgating souls come to an end today.
[19]	Lucifero	Contro il re dell'Averno, anzi dell'ombre, contro il potente nume, chi cotanto presume?	Against the King of the Depths, nay of the Shadows, against the powerful god, who presumes so much?
	Angelo	Alla voce, al splendore a te ben noto, ancor non scorgi, o rio, un ministro di Dio?	By the voice, by the splendor to you well known, can you not yet perceive, oh wicked one, a minister of God?
[20]	Anima [S]	Qual soccorso improvviso?	Oh, what sudden succor?
[21]	Anime	Sembra fatto l'Inferno un Paradiso!	Hell seems turned into a Paradise!
[22]	Angelo	Sù, sù, spariscano, sù, sù, svaniscano l'aspre pene, i rii tormenti.	Away, away, let them disappear; away, away, let them vanish, the bitter pains, the cruel torments.

| | | Voi liete godete,
bell'alme beate,
e meco volate
del Cielo ai contenti. | You happy, beautiful souls be merry and fly with me to the bliss of heaven. |

Sù, sù, spariscano,
sù, sù, svaniscano
l'aspre pene, i rii tormenti.

Away, away, let them disappear; away, away, let them vanish, the bitter pains, the cruel torments.

[23] Del gran motor delle rotanti sfere,
tra l'angeliche schiere,
a vostra sorte
eletto messaggier di conforto,
sopra penne propizie
a voi mi porto.
Si sciolgan le catene
che v'inceppan tra le ombre.
Ogni pena si sgombre,
ch'a forza di preghiere
la pietà dei mortali
per volarvene al Ciel
v'impenna le ali.

I come to you from the great Mover of the rotating spheres, from the midst of angelic hosts, as messenger of comfort on your behalf, upon propitious wings. Let the chains that bind you among the shadows be broken! Let every pain vanish, because by the force of prayers the pity of mortals gives you wings to fly to heaven.

[24] Lucifero   Fiero dolor!   Oh fearful grief!

Anima[S]   Soccorso inaspettato!   Oh unexpected help!

[25] Anime   Rende dolce ogni pena Iddio placato.   Having placated God renders sweet each pain.

[26] Angelo   A cor supplicante, pietoso,
il Tonante resister non sa,
no, resister non sa.

To a supplicant, merciful heart, the Thundering One knows not how to resist.

Con flebili stille, pupille dolenti
son troppo possenti
a muover pietà.

Eyes that suffer from tears of crying are too powerful in moving to pity.

A cor supplicante, pietoso,
il Tonante resister non sa,
no, resister non sa.

To a supplicant, merciful heart, the Thundering One knows not how to resist.

[27] Lucifero   E sì brevi dolori
bastano ai loro errori,
mentre una colpa sola
me con eterno esiglio
al Cielo invola?

And such brief pain is enough for their sins, while a single fault steals heaven from me, to eternal exile?

[28] Angelo	Empio, chiudi quei labri! Ogni castigo alle tue colpe è lieve, ma per alme sì belle, che qual da brevi macchie è tinto il sole, sol da piccioli nei contrasser l'ombre; dal pregar dei mortali vinta l'onnipotenza, ogni giusto rigor cangia in clemenza.	Impious One, close those lips! Any punishment is light for your guilt, but these are beautiful souls that, just as the sun is stained with light spots, have been marred by no more than blemishes. For such souls the Omnipotent One is won through the prayers of mortals and changes every just rigor to clemency.
[29] Anime	Alle gioie, ai contenti! Addio fiamme, addio pene, addio tormenti!	To the joys, to the bliss! Goodbye flames, goodbye pains, goodbye torments!
[30] Ritornello		
[31] Lucifero	Per non mirar, ahi lasso! nei godimenti loro il proprio duolo, entro gl'ardor precipitoso volo.	I cannot bear to look, oh me, upon my defeat in their rejoicing, so I fly away in a hurry through the fire.
[32] Angelo and Anime	Alle gioie, al Paradiso, ai contenti! Già serene giran l'ore dell'ardore, già svaniscono le pene, e dopo un breve pianto eterno è il riso.	To the joys, to Paradise, to the bliss. The hours of our love already revolve serene, already the sufferings vanish, and after a brief cry, laughter is eternal.

Score of *Esule dalle sfere*

[1] *Sinfonia*

[I]

46

[3]*

Mie schie- re se - ve - re, ven- det - ta! Sù, sù! Mie

---

* Designated *aria* in Mus. F. 1148.

[4]

[5]

Coro d'Anime

[8]*

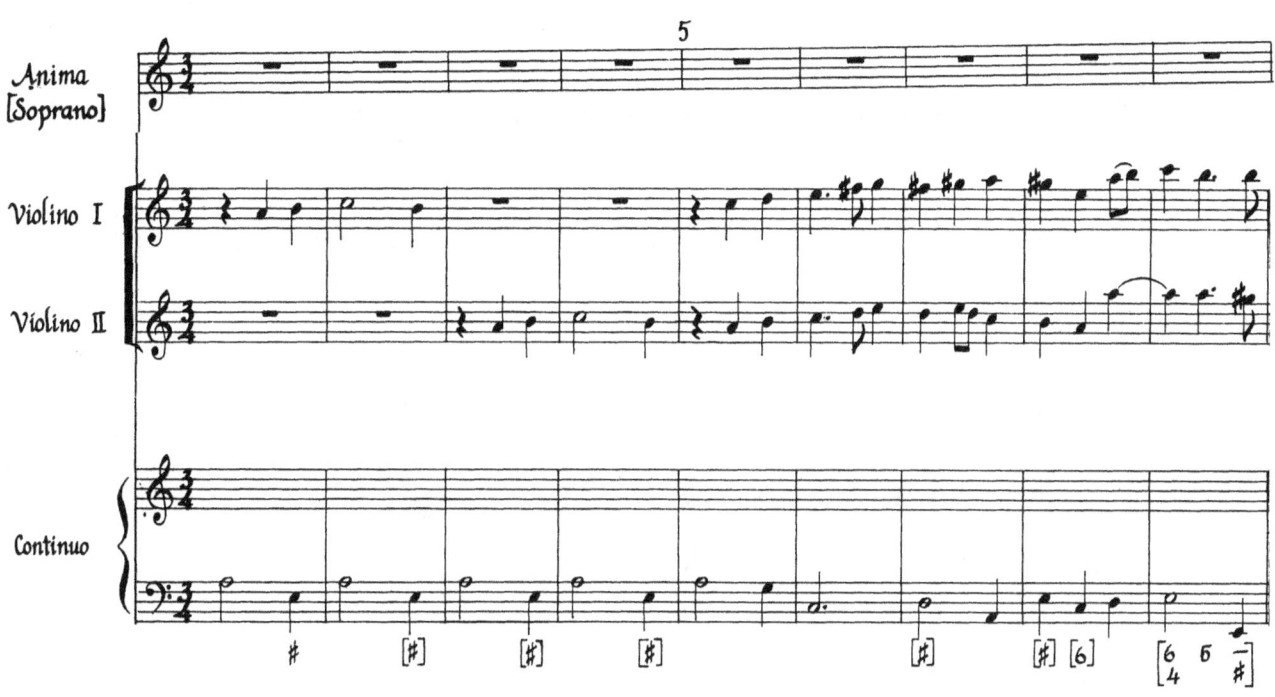

* Designated *aria* in Mus. F. 1148.

[9]

[11a]*

* Sections 11a and 11b are in Mus. F. 1148 only.

* 19–22: In repetition in mm. 29–32, "irato" is used.

[14]

[15] Ritornello

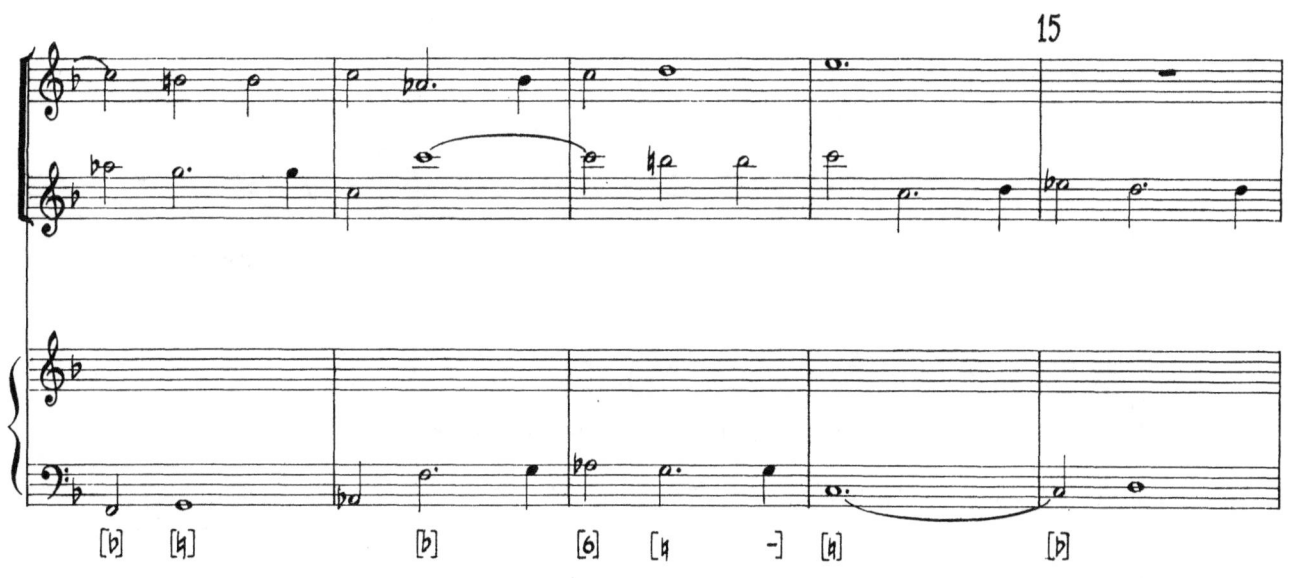

[16]

88

[17]

[18]

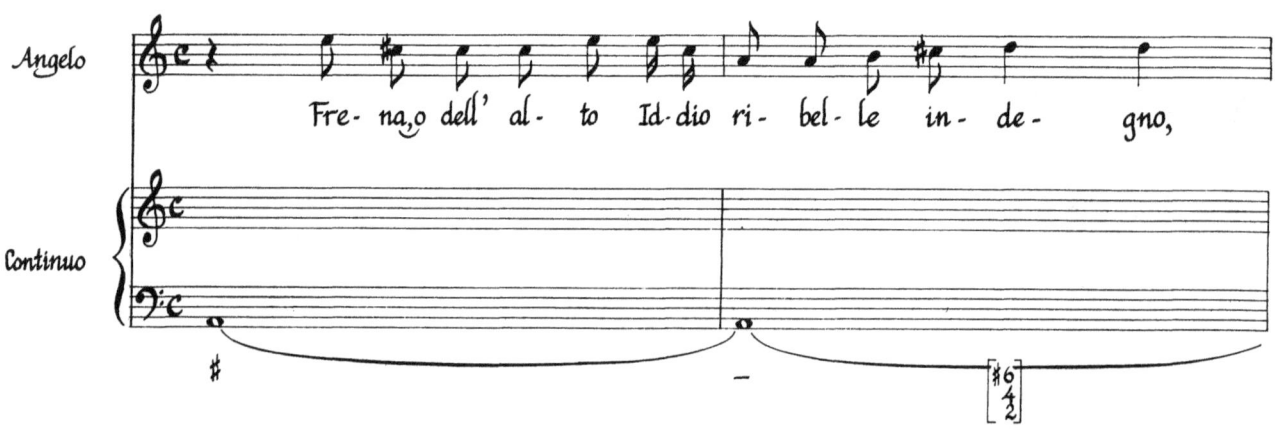

[19]

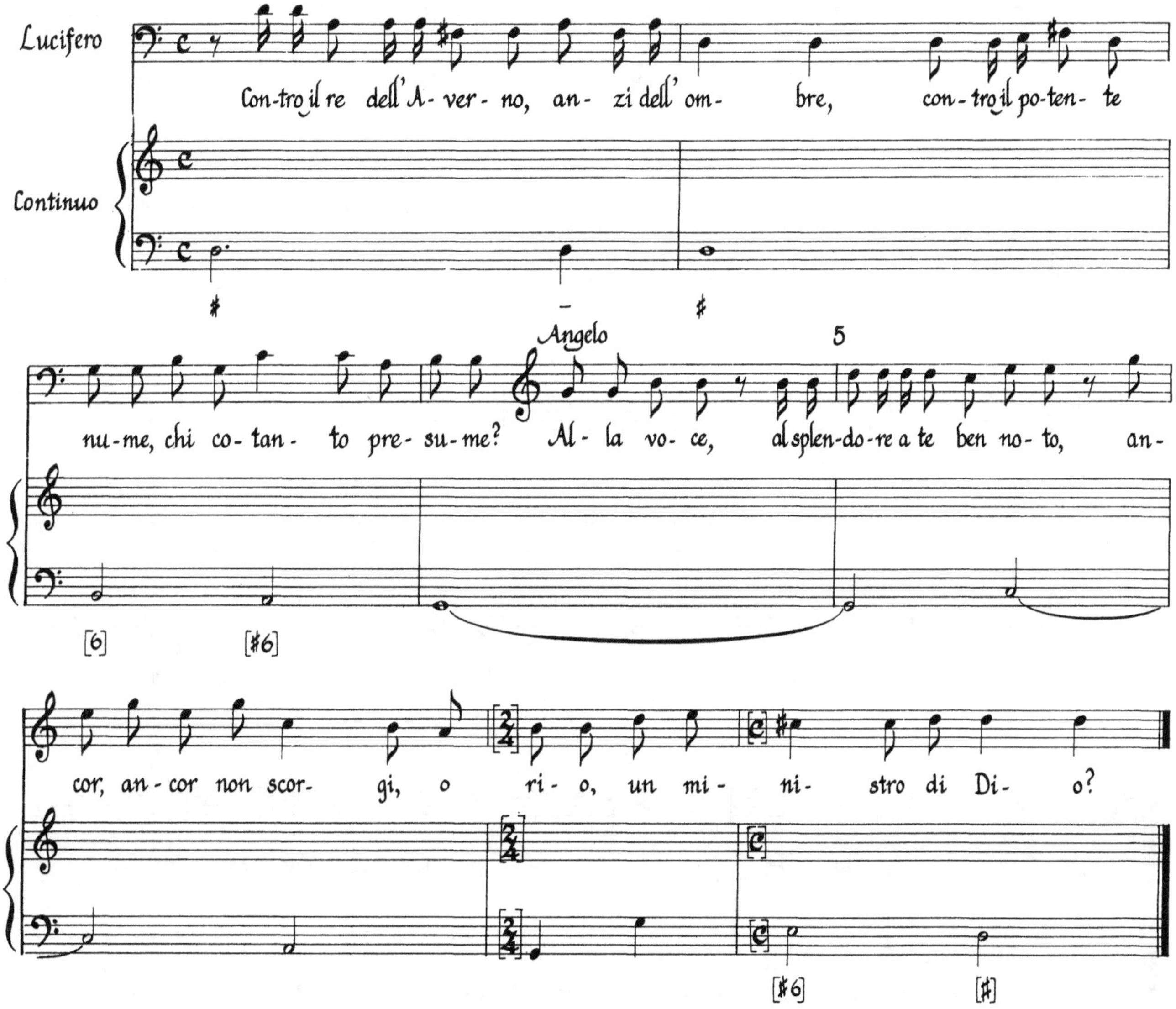
Lucifero
Con-tro il re dell'A-ver-no, an-zi dell'om-bre, con-tro il po-ten-te
Continuo
nu-me, chi co-tan-to pre-su-me?
Angelo
5
Al-la vo-ce, al splen-do-re a te ben no-to, an-
cor, an-cor non scor-gi, o ri-o, un mi-ni-stro di Di-o?
[6]
[#6]
[#6]
[#]

[20]

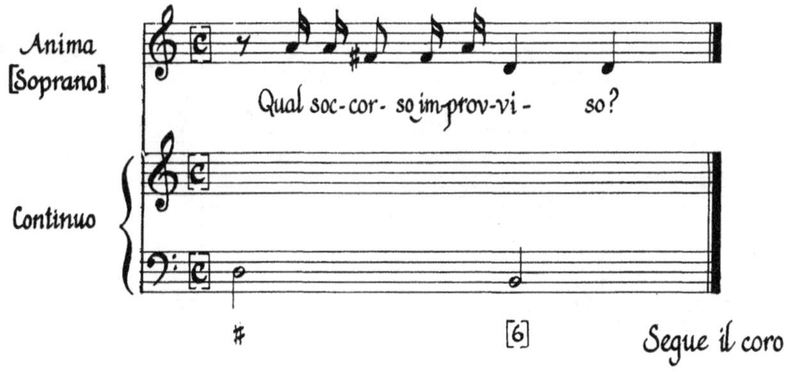
Anima
[Soprano]
Qual soc-cor-so im-prov-vi-so?
Continuo
[6]
Segue il coro

[21]

[22]*

Sù, sù, spa-ri-sca-no, sù, sù, svà-ni-sca-no

* Designated *aria* in Mus. F. 1148.

94

[23]

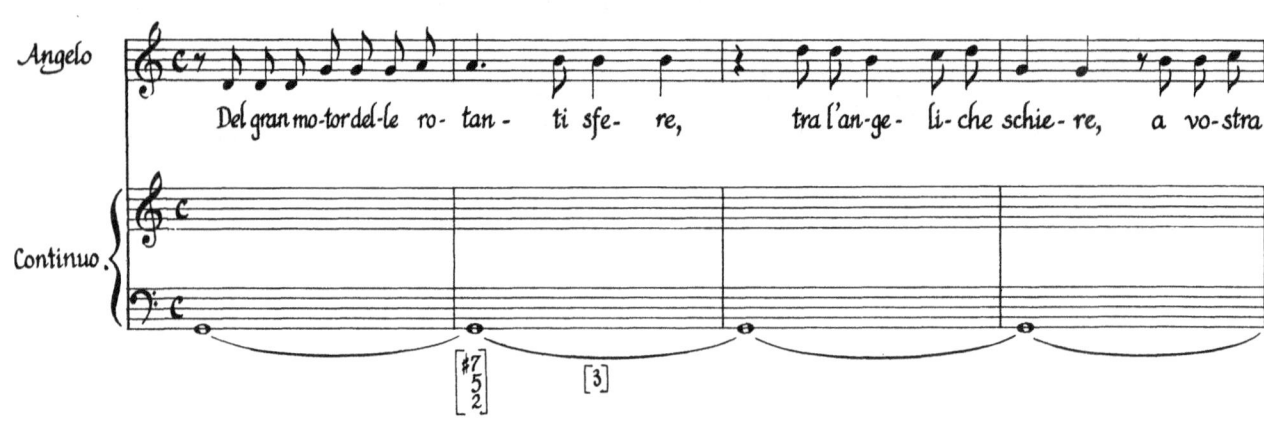

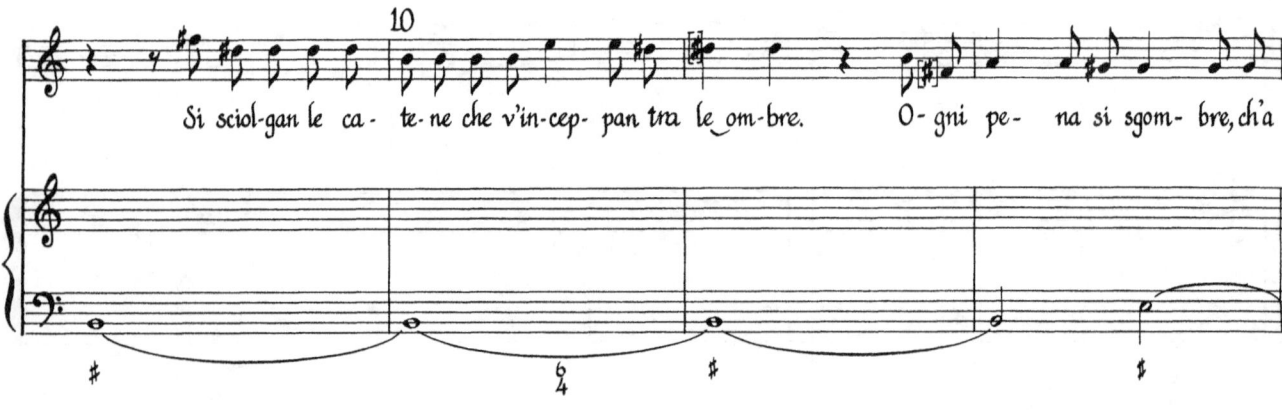

[24]

[25]

106

[26]*

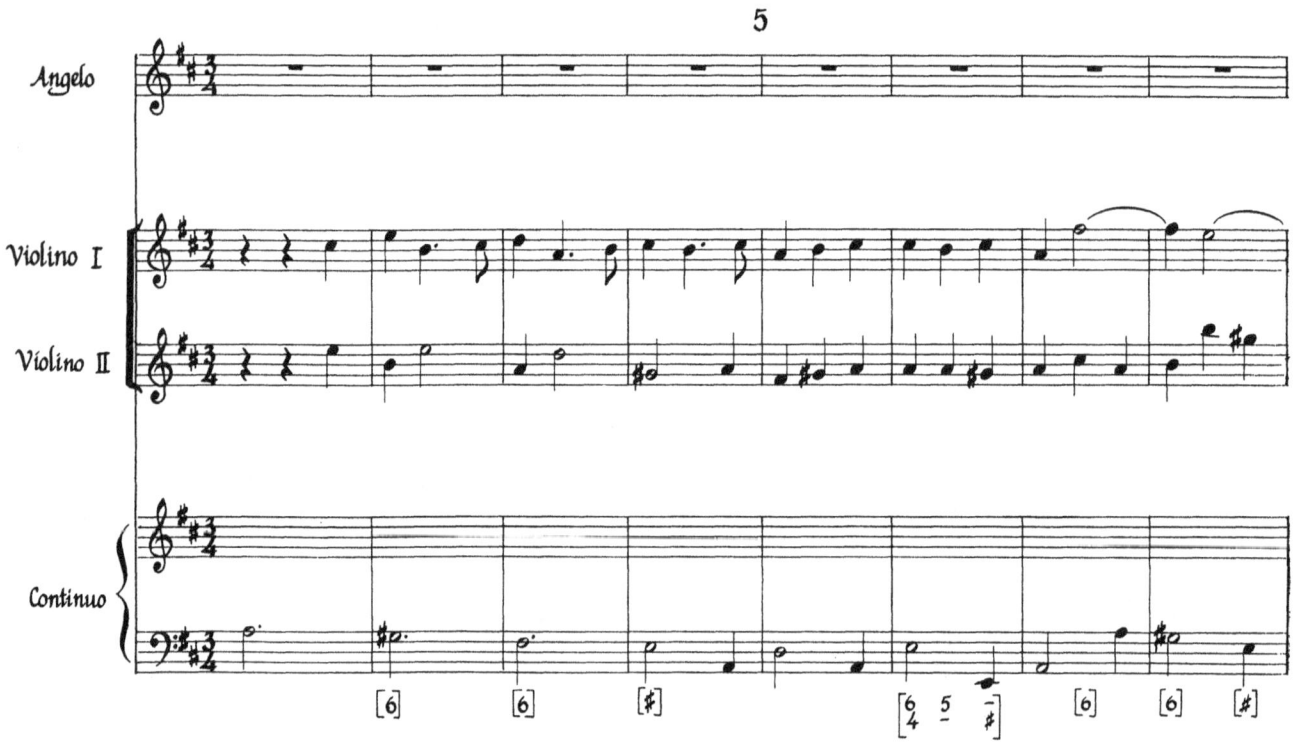

* Designated *aria* in Mus. F. 1148.

[27]

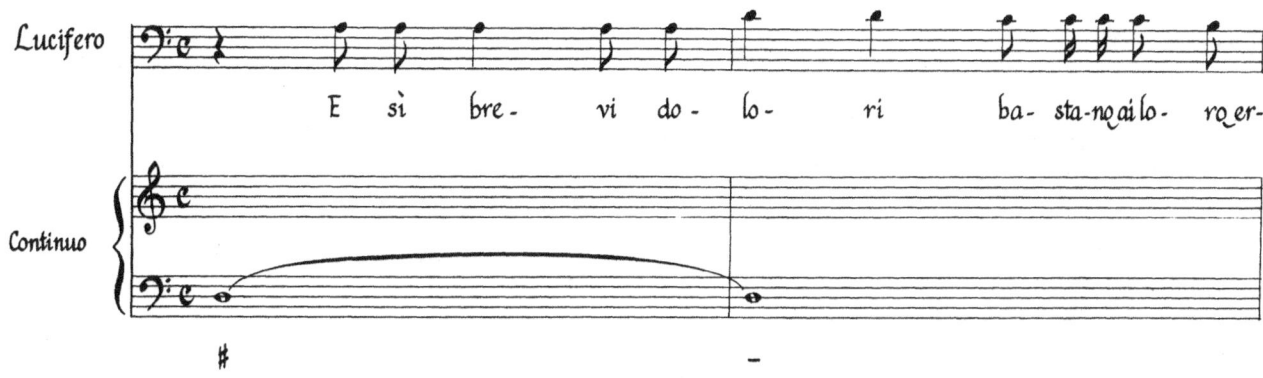

[28]

118

[30] Ritornello

[32]

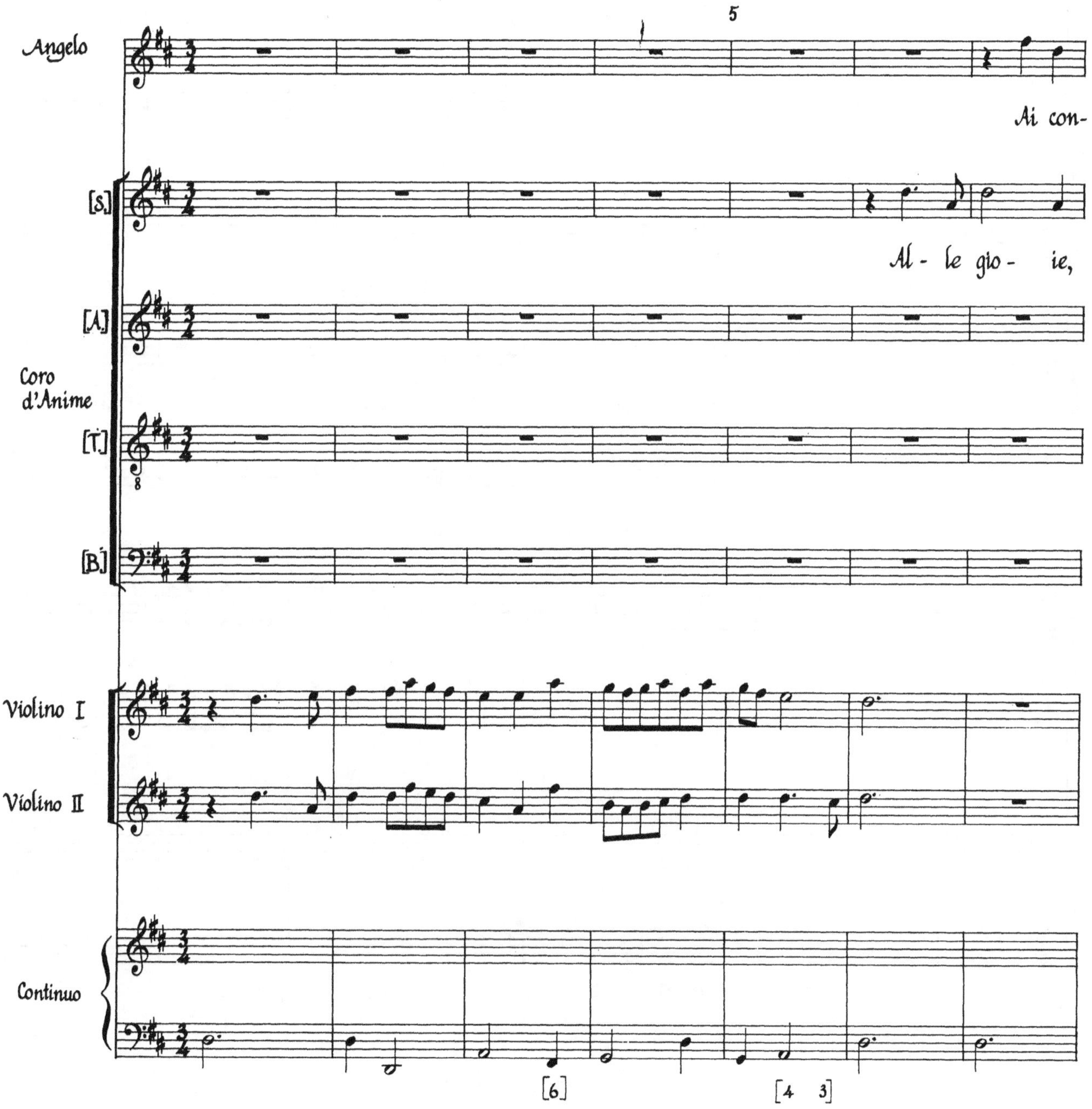
5
Angelo
Ai con-
[S]
Al - le gio - ie,
[A]
Coro d'Anime
[T]
[B]
Violino I
Violino II
Continuo
[6]
[4 3]

Bibliography

Ademollo, Alessandro. *I teatri di Roma nel secolo decimosettimo*. Rome: Loreto Pasqualucci, 1888.

Arnold, Frank Thomas. *The Art of Accompaniment from a Thorough-Bass as Practised in the XVIIth and XVIIIth Centuries*. London: Oxford University Press, 1931.

Bernstein, Harry Marvin. "Alessandro Stradella's Serenata *Il barcheggio* (Genoa, 1681): A Modern Edition and Commentary." 2 vols. D.M.A. dissertation, Stanford University, 1979.

Bonta, Stephen. "On the Track of the Early Violoncello: A Question of Strings?" *Journal of the American Musical Instruments Society* 3 (1976): 64–99.

Borgir, Tharald. "The Performance of the Basso Continuo in Seventeenth Century Italian Music." Ph.D. dissertation, University of California at Berkeley, 1971.

Boyden, David D. *The History of Violin Playing from Its Origins to 1761 and Its Relationship to the Violin and Violin Music*. London: Oxford University Press, 1965.

Bridges, David M. "The Social Setting of *Musica da camera* in Rome: 1667–1700." Ph.D. dissertation, George Peabody College for Teachers, 1976.

Brossard, Sébastien de. *Dictionarie de musique*. 1703. Reprint. Amsterdam: Antiqua, 1964.

Buelow, George J. "The Full-voiced Style of Thorough-bass Realization." *Acta musicologica* 35 (1963): 159–71.

_____. *Thorough-Bass Accompaniment According to Johann David Heinichen*. Berkeley and Los Angeles: University of California Press, 1966.

Burrows, David L. "The Cantatas of Antonio Cesti." Ph.D. dissertation, Brandeis University, 1961.

Caluori, Eleanor. *The Cantatas of Luigi Rossi*. 2 vols. Ann Arbor: UMI Research Press, 1981.

Calvoli, Giovanni Cinelli. *Biblioteca volante*. 4 vols. Venice: Presso Giambattista Albrizzi Q. Girolamo, 1734–47.

Cametti, Alberto. *Il teatro di Tordinona, poi di Apollo*. 2 vols. Tivoli: Arti Grafichi Aldo Chicca, 1938.

Casimiri, Raffaele. "Oratorii del Masini, Bernabei, Melani, Di Poi, Pasquini, e Stradella, in Roma, nell'anno santo 1675." *Note d'archivio per la storia musicale* 13 (1936): 157–69.

Catelani, Angelo. *Delle opere di Alessandro Stradella esistenti nell'Archivio Musicale della R. Biblioteca Palatina di Modena*. Modena: Per Carlo Vincenzi, 1866.

Chaikin, Kathleen Ann. "The Solo Soprano Cantatas of Alessandro Stradella." Ph.D. dissertation, Stanford University, 1975.

Crescimbeni, Giovanni Mario. *L'Arcadia*. Rome: Per Antonio de' Rossi, 1711.

_____. *L'istoria della volgar poesia*. 3d ed. 6 vols. Venice: Lorenzo Basegio, 1730–31.

_____. *Le vite degli Arcadi illustri*. 3 vols. Rome: Nella Stamperia di Antonio de Rossi alla Piazza di Ceri, 1710.

Daniels, David W. "Alessandro Stradella's Oratorio *San Giovanni Battista*—A Modern Edition and Commentary." 2 vols. Ph.D. dissertation, State University of Iowa, 1963.

Dent, Edward J. "Italian Chamber Cantatas." *The Musical Antiquary* 2 (1911): 142–53, 185–99.

Dietz, Hanns-Bertold. "Musikalische Struktur und Architektur im Werke Alessandro Stradellas." *Analecta musicologica* 9 (1970): 78–93.

Donington, Robert. *The Interpretation of Early Music*. 2d ed. London: Faber and Faber, 1975.

_____. *A Performer's Guide to Baroque Music*. New York: Charles Scribner's Sons, 1973.

_____. *String Playing in Baroque Music*. New York: Charles Scribner's Sons, 1977.

Einstein, Alfred. *The Italian Madrigal*. Translated by Alexander H. Krappe, Roger H. Sessions, and Oliver Strunk. 3 vols. Princeton: Princeton University Press, 1949.

Eisley, Irving R. "The Secular Cantatas of Mario Savioni (1608–1685)." Ph.D. dissertation, University of California at Los Angeles, 1964.

Fortune, Nigel. "Italian Secular Monody from 1600 to 1635: An Introductory Survey." *The Musical Quarterly* 39 (1953): 171–95.

Gasparini, Francesco. *L'armonico pratico al cimbalo* [*The Practical Harmonist at the Harpsichord*]. Venice, 1708. Translated from the Italian by Frank S. Stillings. Edited by David L. Burrows. New Haven: Yale School of Music, 1963.

Gentili, Alberto. "La raccolta di antiche musiche 'Renzo Giordano' alla Biblioteca Nazionale di Torino." *Accademie e biblioteche d'Italia* 4 (1930): 117–25.

Gianturco, Carolyn. "Alessandro Stradella: A True Biography." *The Musical Times* 123 (1982): 756–58.

_____. "Caratteri stilistici delle opere teatrali di Stradella." *Rivista italiana di musicologia* 6 (1971): 211–45.

_____. "The Operas of Alessandro Stradella." Ph.D. dissertation, Oxford University, 1970.

_____. "The Oratorios of Alessandro Stradella." *Proceedings of the Royal Music Association* 101 (1974–75): 45–57.

Giazotto, Remo. *Vita di Alessandro Stradella*. 2 vols. Milan: Curci, 1962.

Grout, Donald J. *A Short History of Opera*. 2d ed. New York: Columbia University Press, 1965.

Hanley, Edwin. "Alessandro Scarlatti's *Cantate da camera*: A Bibliographical Study." Ph.D. dissertation, Yale University, 1963.

Haskell, Francis. *Patrons and Painters: A Study in the Relations between Italian Art and Society in the Age of the Baroque.* 2d ed., rev. and enl. New Haven: Yale University Press, 1980.

Hess, Heinz. *Die Opern Alessandro Stradella's.* Publikationen der Internationalen Musikgesellschaft, ser. 2, no. 3. Leipzig: Breitkopf und Härtel, 1906.

Hubbard, Frank. *Three Centuries of Harpischord Making.* Cambridge: Harvard University Press, 1965.

Jander, Owen. "The *Cantata in accademia*: Music for the Accademia de' Dissonanti and their Duke, Francesco II d'Este." *Rivista italiana di musicologia* 10 (1975): 519–44.

———. *A Catalogue of the Manuscripts of Compositions by Alessandro Stradella found in European and American Libraries.* Rev. ed. Wellesley, Mass.: Wellesley College, 1962.

———. "Concerto Grosso Instrumentation in Rome in the 1660's and 1670's." *Journal of the American Musicological Society* 21 (1968): 168–80.

———. "The Works of Alessandro Stradella Related to the Cantata and the Opera." Ph.D. dissertation, Harvard University, 1962.

Jander, Owen, comp. *Alessandro Stradella.* Wellesley Edition Cantata Index Series (WECIS), fasc. 4. Wellesley, Mass.: Wellesley College, 1969.

Landshoff, Ludwig. "Über das vielstimmige Accompagnement und andere Fragen des Generalbaßspiels." In *Festschrift zum 50. Geburtstag Adolf Sandberger überreicht von seinen Schülern*, pp. 189–208. Munich: Ferdinand Zierfuss, 1918.

Liess, Andreas. "Materialien zur römischen Musikgeschichte des Seicento: Musikerlisten des Oratorio San Marcello, 1664–1725." *Acta musicologica* 29 (1957): 137–71.

McCrickard, Eleanor F., ed. *Alessandro Stradella: Instrumental Music.* Concentus musicus, vol. 5. Cologne: Arno Volk Verlag Hans Gerig KG, 1980.

———. "Temporal and Tonal Aspects of Alessandro Stradella's Instrumental Music." *Analecta musicologica* 19 (1979): 186–243.

Marx, Hans Joachim. "Die Musik am Hofe Pietro Kardinal Ottobonis unter Arcangelo Corelli." *Analecta musicologica* 5 (1968): 104–77.

Die Musik in Geschichte und Gegenwart (MGG). Edited by Friedrich Blume. 14 vols. and 2 supps. to date. Kassel: Bärenreiter, 1949–.

Natali, Giulio, ed. *Storia letteraria d'italia: il settecento.* 2 vols. Milan: Casa Editrice Dottor Francesco Vallardi, 1929.

The New Grove Dictionary of Music and Musicians. Edited by Stanley Sadie. 6th ed. 20 vols. London: Macmillan and Co., 1980.

Newman, William S. *A History of the Sonata Idea.* 3 vols. Vol. 1, *The Sonata in the Baroque Era.* Vol. 2, *The Sonata in the Classic Era.* Vol. 3, *The Sonata since Beethoven.* Chapel Hill: University of North Carolina Press, 1959–69.

Penna, Lorenzo. *Li primi albori musicali per il principianti della musica figurata.* 3 bks. Bologna, 1672; reprinted in 1674, 1678 (bk. 2), 1679, 1684, 1696. Reprint of 1684 impression. Bologna: Forni, n.d.

Piantanida, Sandro; Diotallevi, Lamberto; and Livraghi, Giancarlo, comps. *Autori italiani del seicento: Catalogo bibliografico.* 4 vols. Milan: Libereria Vinciana, 1948–49.

Pirrotta, Nino. "Early Opera and Aria." In *New Looks at Italian Opera: Essays in Honor of Donald J. Grout*, edited by William W. Austin, pp. 39–107. Ithaca: Cornell University Press, 1968.

Pitoni, Giuseppe Ottavio. "Alessandro Stradella." In "Notizie de' contrapuntisti e compositori di musica." Manuscript. Rome. Biblioteca Vaticana. Cappella Giulia MS I-2(1).

Prunières, Henry. "The Italian Cantata of the XVII Century." *Music and Letters* 7 (1926): 38–48, 120–32.

Reese, Gustave. *Music in the Renaissance.* Rev. ed. New York: W. W. Norton, 1959.

Rose, Gloria. "The Cantatas of Carissimi." Ph.D. dissertation, Yale University, 1959.

———. "The Cantatas of Giacomo Carissimi." *The Musical Quarterly* 48 (1962): 204–15.

———. "A Fresh Clue from Gasparini on Embellished Figured-Bass Accompaniment." *Musical Times* 107 (1966): 28–29.

———. "The Italian Cantata of the Baroque Period." In *Gattungen der Musik in Einzeldarstellungen: Gedenkschrift Leo Schrade*, edited by Wulf Arlt, Ernst Lichtenhahn, and Hans Oesch, pp. 655–77. Bern and Munich: Francke Verlag, 1973.

Sartori, Claudio. *Giacomo Carissimi: Catalogo delle opere attribuite.* Milan: Finarte, 1975.

Schmitz, Eugen. *Geschichte der Kantate und des geistlichen Konzerts.* Pt. 1, *Geschichte der weltlichen Solokantate.* 2d ed. Leipzig: Breitkopf und Härtel, 1955.

Smither, Howard E. *A History of the Oratorio.* 2 vols. to date. Vol. 1, *The Oratorio in the Baroque Era: Italy, Vienna, Paris.* Vol. 2, *The Oratorio in the Baroque Era: Protestant Germany and England.* Chapel Hill: University of North Carolina Press, 1977–.

Tiraboschi, Girolamo. *Storia della letteratura italiana.* 16 vols. Florence: Presso Molini, Landi e C.º, 1805–13.

Tosi, Pier Francesco. *Opinioni de' cantori antichi, e moderni, o sieno osservazioni sopra il canto figurato [Observations on the Florid Song].* Bologna: Lelio dalla Volpe, 1723. Translated from the Italian by J. E. Galliard. London: Wilcox, 1743.

Veracini, Francesco Maria. "Il trionfo della pratica musicali," op. 3, pt. 2 (entitled "Cronichetta ovvero memorie musicali"). Manuscript. Florence. Conservatorio di musica "Luigi Cherubini." MS 2360.

Wessely-Kropik, Helene. *Lelio Colista, ein römischer Meister vor Corelli: Leben und Umwelt*. Österreichischen Akademie der Wissenschaften, Philosophisch-Historische Klasse, Sitzungsbericht, vol. 237, treatise 4. Veröffentlichungen der Kommission für Musikforschung, edited by Erich Schenk, bk. 3. Vienna: Hermann Böhlaus, 1961.

Whenham, E. John. "Italian Secular Duets and Dialogue c. 1600 to 1643." Ph.D. dissertation, Oxford University, 1978.

Williams, Peter. *Figured Bass Accompaniment*. 2 vols. Edinburgh: Edinburgh University Press, 1970.

———. "The Harpsichord Acciaccatura: Theory and Practice in Harmony, 1650–1750." *The Musical Quarterly* 54 (1968): 503–23.

Ziino, Agostino. "Osservazioni sulla struttura de *L'Accademia d'Amore* di Alessandro Stradella." *Chigiana* 26–27 (1969–70): 137–69.

Index

Agazzari, Agostino, 23n
Agostini, Pietro Simone, 12
Ah! troppo è ver (Stradella), 4, 5n, 14n, 21
Alexander VII (pope), 11. *See also* Chigi, Fabio
Alexander VIII (pope), 6
Alle selve, agli studii (Stradella), 5n
Aloneo, Gomero, 7
Arcadia, 6, 7
Archlute, 22
Aria, 16, 17–18, 28; characteristics of style, 12, 14
Arioso: characteristics of style, 12, 14, 16
L'armonico pratico al cimbalo (Gasparini), 23

Bacilly, Bénigne de, 28
Baldini, Sebastiano, 7
Balducci, Francesco, 15
Banchieri, Adriano, 23n
Barberini, Maffeo, 11
Barberini family, 11
Il barcheggio (Stradella), 4
Baruffaldi, Girolamo, 7
Basso continuo (for *Esule dalle sfere*): scoring of, 16; selection of instruments for, 20–22; sources for realization of, 22–24; written-out realizations of, 23–24; and relationship of realization to vocal line, 24–25; style of realization, 25–26; full-voiced realization of, 25
Berardi, Angelo, 10
Bernabei, Ercole, 3
Berti, Giovanni Pietro, 10
Bianciardi, Francesco, 23n
Bologna, 3, 22
Bononcini, Giovanni, 23
Bononcini, Giovanni Maria, 21
Bonta, Stephen, 22
Borgir, Tharald, 20
Boyd, Malcolm, 9
Brignole-Sale, Anton, 4, 30

Caccini, Giulio, 11, 28
Caldara, Antonio, 15

Cantade et arie a voce sola (Grandi), 9
Cantata, 14, 15, 23; and Stradella's works in the genre of, 4–5, 21; history of genre, 9–13
Cantate da camera a voce sola, op. 1 (Gasparini), 21, 22, 24, 28
Caproli, Carlo, 12
Carissimi, Giacomo, 12, 14, 15
Castrato, 26, 31
Cazzati, Maurizio, 3
Cesti, Antonio, 12
Chigi, Fabio, 11
Chigi family, 11
Choral sections (in *Esule dalle sfere*), 16, 18, 24
Christina (queen of Sweden), 3, 6, 11
Cibo, Cardinal Alderan, 3
Clement IX (pope), 11. *See also* Rospigliosi, Giulio
Colista, Lelio, 21
Colonna, Giovanni Paolo, 15
Colonna family, 3
Concerti morali e spirituali (Savioni), 12, 14
Concerto, 14
Concerto grosso: instrumentation for, 4–5, 5, 14
Corelli, Arcangelo, 23, 25
Corispero (Stradella), 7
Crescembeni, Giovanni Mario, 6, 7, 10
Crivellati, Domenico, 10
Crudo mar di fiamme orribili (Stradella), 5n, 7, 21n

Da cuspide ferrate (Stradella), 5n, 21n
Da sventura a sventura (Alessandro Scarlatti), 23, 24
Della Valle, Pietro, 15
Dialogo, 14
Durazzo family, 29–30

Einstein, Alfred, 10
Este, Francesco II d', 30
Ester, liberatrice del popolo ebreo (Stradella), 21n

Esule dalle sfere: as a cantata, 4–5, 15; as an oratorio, 15; summary of libretto, 16; performance of, 20–28; scoring for, 21; manuscript sources of, 29–30; evaluation of, 30; editorial procedures for performing edition of, 30–31; libretto of, 33–38. *See also* Basso continuo; Choral sections; Instrumental sections; Performance practices; Style, characteristics of

Falanzio, Montano, 6
Ferretto, Arturo, 7n
Figari, Pompeo, 29, 33; biography and works of, 6–8
Florence, 3, 11
Fortune, Nigel, 9

Gamba, 20, 22
Gasparini, Francesco, 20–21, 22, 23, 24, 25, 28
Genoa, 4, 6, 7, 8, 9, 29–30
Gianturco, Carolyn, 3n
Giordano, Filippo, 29–30
Grandi, Alessandro, 9, 10

Handel, George Frideric, 4n, 15
Hanley, Edwin, 12
Harpsichord, 20, 21, 23; Italian, 25; and characteristics of style, 25–26
Heinichen, Johann, 25
Hor ch'alla dea notturna (Stradella), 26–27

Innocent XI (pope), 3, 6, 11. *See also* Odescalchi, Benedetto
Instrumental music: works by Stradella, 8n, 21, 28, 29
Instrumental sections (in *Esule dalle sfere*), 16, 18–19

Jander, Owen, 4, 5

Legrenzi, Giovanni, 15
Lomellini family, 4

Madrigal, 10, 13
Marazzoli, Marco, 12, 15
Marciani, Giovanni, 12
Marino, Giambattista, 11
Mazzocchi, Domenico, 12, 15
Mazzocchi, Virgilio, 12
Melani, Atto, 12
Michi, Orazio, 12
Milanuzzi, Carlo, 10
Minato, Nicolò, 7
Modena, 26, 29–30
Monesio, Giovanni Pietro, 7
Monody, 10
Monteverdi, Claudio, 10, 28

Negri, Francesco, 10
Nepi, 3
Neri, Philip, 13
Nettunio, Cluento, 7
Norcia, Antonio Domenico, 7

Odescalchi, Benedetto, 3, 6, 11
Odescalchi, Signor D. Livio, 6
Opinioni de' cantori antichi (Tosi), 28
Oratorio, 9, 21; history of genre, 13–15
Organ, 20, 21, 23
L'ottavo libro de madrigali (Wert), 10
Ottoboni, Pietro, 6, 7

Pamphilj family, 11
Pasqualini, Marc'Antonio, 12
Pasquini, Bernardo, 12, 23
Penna, Lorenzo, 23, 24, 25, 28
Performance practices (for *Esule dalle sfere*): size of chorus, 26; selection of voices, 16, 26; tempo, 17, 28; selection of instruments, 20–22; realization of the continuo, 22–24; ornamentation, 26–28; trills, 26, 28; appoggiaturas, 28; cadenzas, 28
Pesenti, Martino, 10
Pirrotta, Nino, 26

Praetorius, Michael, 23n, 25
Pugna certamen (Stradella), 4, 5n, 21
Purcell, Henry, 21

Qual prodigio è ch'io miro (Stradella), 4
Il quinto libro de madrigali (Monteverdi), 10

Ragionamenti musicali (Berardi), 10
Recitatives, 16–17, 25, 28; characteristics of style, 12, 14
Reese, Gustave, 10
Remarques curieuses sur l'art de bien canter (Bacilly), 28
Rome, 3, 6, 7, 8, 9, 11, 12, 21, 22, 23, 25
Rose, Gloria, 9, 10, 12, 23
Rospigliosi, Giulio, 11
Rossi, Luigi, 12
Rovetta, Giovanni, 10

Sabbatini, Galeazzo, 23n
Sances, Giovanni Felice, 10
San Giovanni Battista (Stradella), 3, 21, 22
San Giovanni Grisostomo (Stradella), 21n
Santa Edita (Stradella), 21n
Santa Pelagia (Stradella), 21n
Savioni, Mario, 12, 12–13, 14
Scarlatti, Alessandro, 12, 15, 23, 24, 25
Scarselli, Rinieri, 10
Schmitz, Eugen, 10
Sereni, Francesco Maria, 7
Si apra al riso ogni labbro (Stradella), 5n, 14n, 21n
Smither, Howard E., 13
Stradella, Alessandro: revision of birth date for, 3; and Roman period of, 3, 12, 15; biography of, 3–4; and patrons of, 3–4; authenticity of cantatas, 4; characteristics of cantatas, 4; secular cantatas of, 4; use of soloists, 4, 16–17, 26; use of the chorus, 4, 18; use of instruments, 4, 18–19, 20–22, 26–27; scoring of cantatas, 4, 20–22; sacred cantatas of, 4–5; catalog of works of, 4–5, 30; and relationship to Pompeo Figari, 7–8; use of ornamentation, 26–28. See also *Esule dalle sfere*; Pompeo Figari; Instrumental music
Style, characteristics of (for *Esule dalle sfere*): structural aspects, 16–19; cadences, 16, 26–27, 28; meter, 17; harmonic aspects, 17, 18, 19; ostinato, 17; melodic aspects, 17–18; word painting, 17–18; rhythmic aspects, 18, 19; contrapuntal writing, 18, 19, 24, 25
La Susanna (Stradella), 18, 21n, 29n
Syntagma musicum (Praetorius), 25

Tante perle (Stradella), 20
Teatro Tordinona, 3
Tenaglia, Antonio Francesco, 12
Timms, Colin, 9
Tonelli, Antonio, 25
Torelli, Giuseppe, 21
Tosi, Francesco, 28
Turin, 3–4, 29, 30
Turini, Francesco, 10

Urban VIII (pope), 11. See also Barberini, Maffeo

Vatican, 26; Apostolic Palace, 13, 14
Venice, 3, 11, 25
Veracini, Francesco Maria, 3
Viadana, Lodovico, 23n
Vinchioni, Cinthio, 7
Violins, 4–5, 16, 20, 21, 22
Violoncello, 20, 22
Vitali, Giovanni Battista, 21
Vivaldi, Antonio, 15

Wendham, John, 9n
Wert, Giaches de, 10

Zazara, Domenico, 7

www.ingramcontent.com/pod-product-compliance
Lightning Source LLC
Chambersburg PA
CBHW081826300426
44116CB00014B/2493